For Martin Wolf—
I hope you find this
interesting.
        Best regards,
        Frank Newman

Six Myths that Hold Back America

And What America Can Learn from the Growth of China's Economy

Frank N. Newman

DIVERSIONBOOKS

2011

Diversion Books
A Division of Diversion Publishing Corp.
80 Fifth Avenue, Suite 1101
New York, New York 10011

www.diversionbooks.com

Library of Congress Cataloging-in-Publication Data
Newman, Frank N.
p.   cm.
First Diversion Books edition November 2011
ISBN: 9-780-9839885-1-9
1. Economic theory—United States 2. Consumption
HB1-3840   2011   310-dc31

1 3 5 7 9 10 8 6 4 2

Contents

Six Myths that Hold Back America

Introduction

At one point in the classic Marx Brothers movie *Duck Soup*, Chico asks: "Who you gonna believe, me or your own eyes?"

Five years leading a Chinese bank were an extraordinary time for me: exciting, complex, educational, frustrating, fun, and ultimately very successful. Shenzhen Development Bank was transformed from a very troubled national bank with low capital, high nonperforming loans, and low profitability, to a highly successful and healthy bank—without any government money. That is another story, and perhaps even another book, but the experience was highly thought-provoking in a number of ways.

I often thought about why the economy of China did so well, even during very challenging times, and in such contrast to the U.S. and other Western economies. My experience at the U.S. Treasury in the 1990s—a very good time for the U.S. economy—helped me identify underlying distinctions in the views of economic issues that were driving policies in the two countries: the economic thought and attitudes in the U.S. and in most Western nations, in contrast to attitudes towards similar aspects of the economy in China.

That line of inquiry led me to focus on some commonly accepted statements about economic matters in the U.S.—views that are not given such attention in China. Although the statements in America and Europe were often from sources which seemed like they should be reliable, the differences from underlying views in China were so great that I was motivated to delve into the statements, so I could believe my "own eyes" and my own mind, led by logic—rather than being led by popular statements, assumptions, or dogma.

This book analyzes several key statements of "accepted" economic views in the U.S., to determine which have real basis in the U.S. financial system and which are really just myths. The resulting theme is that there are six myths in particular that have undermined good economic policy and seriously hampered economic growth in the U.S. The book also outlines how economic development in China has avoided falling victim to these myths and has done extraordinarily well, unfettered by the fears resulting from the myths. My hope is that once the underlying issues are better understood, the development of U.S. policies to foster economic growth can flow much more productively.

This book proceeds by logic. It is not empirical, presenting conclusions based on patterns of data, and it does not start with preconceptions and then try to support them. It does not follow any doctrine or "conservative" or "liberal" political or economic views. It just follows the money—using illustrations of how the money system works and how transactions are done in real banking systems. The conclusions in this book are sometimes very substantially at odds with the "accepted wisdom": the book is structured to address "myths."

This book is oriented toward people who read the business press regularly and have some familiarity with the economic issues. I hope that some readers will be happy to follow the logic, with open minds, to where it leads. Often, the established terminology is very specialized and makes some of the myths seem "obviously true," when in fact they are misunderstood and misleading at best, as can be seen by careful examination of the terms and logic.

The analysis here is oriented toward the U.S. financial and monetary system, but many of the principles apply to any country with its own currency and central bank. As explained in Chapter 6, there is a key difference for the eurozone, which has its own special structure of national governments sharing one currency and one central bank.

Thanks

To my wife, Liz, great appreciation for her continuous support, encouragement, and thoughtful questions.

Thanks to my son, Dan, for his strong insights on many of the issues in this book. Much of the analysis was developed as Dan and I talked through policy questions over the years and worked through some of the most challenging aspects of the logic and the implications.

Frank Newman
August, 2011

Prologue

America and China in the Coming Year

A t the start of 2011, the United States of America and the People's Republic of China faced some similar economic challenges: the need to create millions of jobs, the danger of GDP running well below capacity, and the challenges of preparing for the future in a highly competitive global economy.

Let's envision, just past the end of this year. **January, 2012:** representatives of these two great economies appear before an international forum to review their accomplishments in 2011.

First, the representatives from the United States:

"During the year 2011, U.S. economic policy primarily focused on virtuous economic behavior, trying to avoid some of the practices that have come to be widely recognized in America as bad. Austerity was our watchword. We tried to avoid public financing crowding out good business investment projects in the financial markets. We tried to reduce our nation's dependence on foreign funding. We tried to increase national Saving by encouraging consumers and governments at every level to spend less, and by trying to reduce the federal deficit, to avoid leaving great burdens for our children. At the end, the nation was able to produce growth in GDP of about 2 percent for the year. True, that was a relatively low figure after a recession. True, few new jobs were created. True, unemployment stayed well above 8 percent. True, we did not make much progress in updating our aging infrastructure of roads and bridges that need repair, dams that are wearing away, airports without sufficient capacity, and electrical distribution systems that are subject to risk and not well prepared for growth. True, America's real GDP narrowly surpassed the level set in 2007, even after four years. But we are hopeful that if we continue to follow the virtuous economic path of austerity and avoid what we believe to be bad practices, that America will once again show its great strength of development for the future."

Next, the representatives from China:

"During this past year the economy of China grew at over 8 percent, as it has for each of the past 12 years. GDP in 2011 was 40 percent higher, in real terms, than in 2007. Millions of new jobs were created. Substantial infrastructure was built for future use. China's economic activity has not been held back by concerns expressed by our American colleagues. Our methods of financing infrastructure are different, and we do not have great focus on all the traditional Western financial measures and judgments. The money supply in China has grown over 15 percent, properly supporting growth of the economy. We recognize that, although Chinese people tend to save, saving does not create economic activity; we have encouraged consumer confidence and growth in spending in the consumer sector. We encouraged businesses to expand and modernize their productive capacity. And we recognize that without government initiatives the economy would run well below capacity. We have been investing heavily in infrastructure, including highways, bridges, high-speed railways, airports, electrical grids, and ports, at the same time giving increased attention to environmental improvements. Our programs have been large, relative to China's GDP. Like Americans, we have been concerned about what we believe will be economically good for our children—but we have reached different conclusions. During this past year we have developed a stronger economy, with further gifts to future generations, including expanded educational facilities and programs, and modern, productive infrastructure that we and our children can use effectively to produce efficiently in the upcoming years of the global economy."

America Going Forward

Does this contrast truly portray what the future holds for America? The U.S. economy is still the largest in the world, but is running well below capacity and with high unemployment. The differences in this simple exercise are striking: not just the disparity in GDP growth between the countries since 2007, but also the sense that many Americans have of roads and bridges barely keeping up with needed maintenance, compared with strong development of important infrastructure in China. We have to search for a better understanding of how our different approaches are creating vastly different outcomes.

China continues to focus on growth, jobs, and development of infrastructure, using various forms of government-backed financing as a tool to help achieve those goals. The U.S. is now more focused on austerity, limited by a particular set of views, including concerns about financing, especially government deficits. The U.S. is particularly influenced by the difficult times of the recent financial crisis and recession; still, there should be something to be learned from how China, despite its major financing activities, avoided a recession. Perhaps the spirit, entrepreneurship and innovation of Americans will rekindle the economy, regardless of government policies.

But we can try for policies that are likely to help, not hold the economy back.

China's economy has done extremely well not just recently, but for more than 20 years. So let's examine what can be learned from how China has operated so successfully without many of the economic fears of America. Are all the constraints affecting U.S. policy really well-founded? Do they apply at all times, regardless of the state of the economy? How is it possible that the economy in China has done so well without attention to matters that seem so important to many political and opinion leaders in today's America? Are all these commonly held views in the U.S. really based on sound logic, or are some really myths, based on misconceptions and misunderstandings, that are needlessly holding back America?

In that spirit, let us together examine six of the most critical issues for the American economy.

Chapter 1

Myth #1
Asian nations are bankrolling the U.S.

The U.S. as a nation is often characterized as a "borrower" in need of support from Asian "lenders." We hear statements that the U.S. government needs Asian financial support for issuance of Treasury securities and that the U.S. financial system needs dollars to be "returned" from Asia. But when this author has spoken with people in China who have responsibility for investing the dollars, they expressed a very different view: they knew they had dollars, accumulated from trade surpluses, which had to be invested. They were not talking about "lending" to support America. They spoke only about investing the dollars wisely in a complex and competitive global market.[1]

---

[1] In addition, China is very much aware that exports are a key

The myth often portrays the U.S. as a nation and a government dependent on the goodwill of Asian nations in order to avoid "running out of money." It suggests that large amounts of U.S. dollars have been "moved" outside of the U.S., and that the U.S. is in dire need of the return of those dollars to America. Let's look behind those assertions, at the flows of money.

Countries that sell more goods and services to the U.S. than they buy from the U.S. end up with trade surpluses in U.S. dollars. If they really do not want to have U.S. dollar ("USD") assets, they could buy more goods from the U.S. and thus reduce or eliminate the trade surplus with America. But many countries like having such a trade surplus if possible, which means that they will have U.S. dollar assets. What can they do with the dollars they own? The USD money could be left in U.S. bank accounts, as originally received, or invested in various other forms of USD assets.

Fish Live in Water, and U.S. Dollars Live in Banks in the U.S.

Travelers can carry dollar bills across borders, but of course in modern times paper money represents only a small portion of total money and of transactions in

---

part of its economy, providing jobs for millions of workers, and that the U.S. is a major market: China "needs" American customers, who want low-cost goods. This should be the basis of a mutually beneficial relationship.

the banking system. Most transactions are paid using demand deposit accounts (checking accounts) at commercial banks. The banks themselves use accounts at the Federal Reserve banks to hold their "reserves," and to transfer money from bank to bank. We know that the expression "move money" is not really referring to physically moving money—carrying around bags of cash—but it is often misunderstood. Dollars do not actually move to another country. What does change is how many dollars are in which U.S. bank accounts. So for example, if Miss Jones pays Mr. Smith $100 by writing a check to him, and they both have accounts at the same bank, then the bank simply reduces the checking account of Miss Jones by $100 and increases the account of Mr. Smith by the $100. If they have accounts at different banks, then the same result is achieved through the two banks' accounts at the Fed: the account of Miss Jones is reduced and the account of Mr. Smith is increased, by the same $100.

Money is Never Consumed

No money is "used up"; the banking system simply records a change in ownership of that $100. Person A may feel his or her $100 is gone, but it has just been added to another account at a U.S. bank member of the Federal Reserve System. For the U.S. banking system as a whole, the amount of money remains unchanged.

Similarly, when people talk of "moving" money to another country, we know that does not mean transporting huge amounts of hundred dollar bills across the ocean in giant suitcases. In fact, dollars never leave the U.S. (other than the small amount of paper currency carried by travelers). They cannot leave the U.S., by definition. The essence of the U.S. dollar is an obligation of a bank in the United States that has an account with the Fed. So, for example, if an American retailer buys some products from an Asian producer and pays for them with U.S. dollars, the ownership of that block of dollars is recorded as now owned by an Asian account holder instead of an American, at a bank in the U.S. No money is used up, and no money leaves the U.S. When the Fed publishes figures on the U.S. money supply, such as M1 and M2, it adds up the total amount of deposits in all the Fed member banks in the U.S., regardless of which depositors are American or foreign. That is what U.S. dollar money means.

Even if a foreign owner of U.S. dollar deposits thinks of having some of those dollar deposits in a bank in its own country, that is not really quite right. In fact, if a government entity or company or person somewhere in Asia has a bank account denominated in dollars in a local bank, that bank is an intermediary, with an arrangement with a correspondent bank in the U.S. The dollars are actually held at the U.S. bank.[2] The overseas bank and the bank in the U.S. have an agreement under which the U.S. bank holds dollars in a U.S. account for the benefit of the foreign bank. Dollars never leave the U.S.; the amount of dollars in different accounts changes, but dollars cannot leave the U.S. banking system nor be "used up". That leads us to the main conclusions regarding Myth #1...

What Foreigners Can and Cannot Do with U.S. Dollars

When foreigners own dollars from their trade surpluses, there are only three things they can do with the dollars: they can buy American goods and services; they can invest in USD assets; or they can exchange dollars for assets in another currency—in which case the new owner of the dollars will have choices one or two.

When a foreigner buys or sells U.S. dollars, that does not change the total amount of dollars in the system; it simply moves the ownership of a block of dollars from one account owner's U.S. bank account to another. The money supply can be reduced or increased in the U.S. by the Fed, or by banks making loans, but not by the Treasury and not by foreign owners of dollar assets. When the Treasury issues securities, it receives money paid by

---

[2] Or at a registered U.S. office of a foreign bank in the U.S., with an account at the Fed.

investors from their bank accounts, and then distributes the money in the normal course of the Treasury's business, to pay government bills, employees, etc. The Treasury just causes movement of money from one set of bank accounts to other bank accounts, without changing the amount of money in the system. All the dollars get mixed together in the huge U.S. financial system.

Much of the international trade of the U.S. is done in dollars, but even if American companies pay for Asian goods in the currency of the Asian country, the American companies need to exchange dollars for that currency, and someone outside the U.S. ends up owning more dollars. So, for example, if the U.S. company buys $1 million worth of goods from China or Japan, then the U.S. company instructs its bank to take $1 million out of its bank account and put it into the U.S.-based account owned by a Chinese or Japanese entity. The Asian company then has another $1 million in its bank account in the U.S.

If foreign entities with trade surpluses do not want to own U.S. dollar financial assets, then they could buy more goods and services from America; that would be quite fine. But as long as they are selling more to the U.S. than they are buying, they have to end up holding more dollars.

If they still have dollars in their bank accounts, then what might they do with the dollars? They could just leave them in their bank accounts in U.S., which would earn little or no interest. More likely, they will decide to buy some U.S. dollar assets that they expect will produce the risk/reward return of their choice. They might decide to buy corporate bonds or stocks, but if they choose assets with minimal risk, they would invest in U.S. Treasury securities. If they opt to buy corporate bonds, then their dollars will be transferred to the current owners of those bonds, who will then have the dollars in their bank accounts. Those people will then be faced with the decision of what to do with the dollars in the bank. They may buy another asset from someone else, but eventually somebody has those dollars in their bank account, and someone who wants low-risk USD assets will decide to invest it in Treasury securities. Investment in U.S. Treasuries is extremely broad around the world. The U.S. is not a "needy borrower"; quite to the contrary: U.S. Treasuries are the primary choice for investors who want the safest places for their dollars.

A foreign holder of the dollars could decide he prefers to own a different currency. In that case, he would buy the other currency from someone else, and those dollars would be transferred into that other person's account at a U.S. bank. (This process might place downward pressure on the dollar exchange rates; however, it is not clear how much effect it might have, with foreign exchange trading now in excess of $4 trillion per day, and with many international transactions, including oil, denominated in

U.S. dollars.) The buyer of the dollars would then invest them in USD assets. In the case of newly issued Treasuries, the Treasury is depositing an equivalent amount of dollars in U.S. bank accounts, and someone has those dollars and will want to do something with them. But in any case, somebody would end up holding those dollars in U.S. financial assets, and again, as the market clears, someone who wants low-risk USD assets would buy the U.S. Treasuries.

The key point is that when a country sells more goods and services to the U.S. than it buys from America, it will have U.S. bank accounts with U.S. dollars that have to be invested someplace. In an extreme case, if the foreign owners of the USD bank account just left the $1 million in the U.S. bank, then the bank would have an additional $1 million to invest. If the bank simply left the $1 million in its excess reserve account at the Fed, the earnings for the bank would be very small, and the bank itself could well choose to buy Treasuries instead, using the dollars left in the account. This is further explained in Chapter 6: the Fed could easily adjust the interest rate on excess reserves to encourage banks to buy more Treasuries; in any event, the money must stay in the U.S. financial system, and some investors will always have the dollars to buy the Treasuries.

In the end of the sequence of transactions, some investors who have the extra USD cash in their bank accounts will not want to add more corporate risk to their port-folios. They have a choice between just leaving the cash in U.S. bank deposits, which earn very little, if any, inter-est, and are not guaranteed by the government (beyond $250,000)[3], or buying the Treasuries, which have the "full faith and credit" of the U.S. government.

Four Related Myths

Myth 1.1: Excessive savings flows from Asia harm America

We often hear statements suggesting that "money from savings of Asians has been flowing to the U.S. and Eu-rope, and that high levels of money saved in Asian coun-tries has led to a glut of savings money globally and specifically for the U.S." But that is not possible. This is not a matter of differing conclusions from study of economic data; it is a matter of how the international money systems actually work: as explained below, it is literally not possible. It's also odd that this myth implies too much money coming from Asia, while the main Myth #1 portrays the U.S. as desperately needing funds from Asia. But let's follow the real flows of money. Domestic savings in another country exist in the currency and fi-nancial system of that nation, thus cannot flow to the U.S. and cannot mean a flood of money in the U.S. As

---

[3] Except for a temporary unlimited guarantee for certain non-in-terest accounts.

noted above, a country might have U.S. dollars in U.S. bank accounts as a result of a trade surplus, but that is a different matter from the amount or percentage of domestic saving in that country. A country with a balanced trade account might have a high saving rate, but that domestic saving cannot be "sent" to the U.S. Statements about Asian countries sending their savings (money) to the U.S. have two fundamental flaws. First, as explained in Chapter 3, economic Saving has a very specialized meaning in this context of GDP, and cannot be transferred between nations.[4] Second, funds in another currency cannot be sent to the U.S. or any other country as an addition to our own U.S. dollar money supply. If a country has an exchangeable currency, then investors in that country could buy some U.S. dollars from somebody, delivering an amount of their own currency in exchange. The sellers of the dollars would simply transfer ownership of them to the new owners, and the sellers of the dollars would now own some assets in currency X instead of owning assets in dollars; the total amount of dollars in the U.S. financial system would not and could not be affected. Whether another country has a high or

---

[4]When thoughtful economists make comments along these lines, they must not be referring to money flowing to the U.S.—they must be noting that Asians spend a smaller proportion of their economic production each year on consumption, compared to the U.S., and generally record trade surpluses. These important differences between money and the economic production terms are discussed in Chapter 3.

low saving rate in its own currency in its own domestic economy has no direct effect on the money supply of the U.S.

China is an especially good example. Suppose that a Chinese worker earns 100,000 Chinese yuan ("renminbi" or "RMB") after tax, and saves 40,000. The idea that he might use some of that 40,000 yuan to buy U.S. Treasuries or any other USD asset is impossible under the currency rules of China. He cannot buy USD assets with renminbi; he would have to convert his 40,000 yuan to U.S. dollars. But the renminbi is not freely convertible. He cannot go to his bank or broker to buy USD assets with yuan, and the currency rules will not allow him to convert his yuan to dollars. So, his 40,000 yuan saving can affect the domestic Chinese economy, but *cannot* become savings applicable to the U.S. China as a country has a trade surplus with the U.S., which means it buys less from America than it sells to America, and receives net payment in U.S. dollars; however, that is not driven and *cannot* be driven by the rate of *domestic* saving of yuan inside China. Chinese earners do tend to save a large portion of their earnings, and that presents certain challenges to Chinese economic management (as discussed in Chapter 9). But that does not determine the trade deficit. As further discussed in Chapter 3, economic Saving for a nation has to equal the sum of domestic Investment and net exports. In recent years in China, Investment has been running at about 45 percent of GDP, and net exports at about 5 percent. The import/export ratio determines a portion of the total economic Saving figure; it's true that if Chinese consumers bought more goods from the U.S., that would reduce the Chinese trade surplus as well as the Saving figure computed for China. But the total money supply in the U.S. would be unaffected; a lower U.S. trade deficit would just mean that a larger proportion of USD assets would be owned by Americans, and the total amount of USD assets would not change. In any case, the bulk of economic Saving in China is domestic. Whether Chinese workers might save more or less of their earnings domestically, in yuan, would have no direct effect on China's trade surplus and no effect on the need for the Chinese government to find places to invest its USD holdings that result from the trade. Even if Saving and domestic Investment decreased or increased by 1 trillion yuan in China, that would have no direct effect on the U.S. money supply.

If we look at domestic Saving in an Asian country that does have a convertible currency, the same conclusion follows: the local Saving cannot be added to the U.S. money system. People in Japan, for example, save relatively high shares of their income, but they cannot use, in the U.S., the yen they have saved in Japan. They could exchange some yen for dollars, which means that some Americans would simply give ownership of some existing dollars in U.S. bank accounts to Japanese investors who would give ownership of yen in Japanese banks to the Americans: there would be no new dollars created, no addition to Saving in the U.S. No one in America could use yen to buy groceries or shoes at the local mall. Neither the money supply of Japan, in yen, nor the money supply of the U.S., in dollars, would change. And neither the Saving of the U.S. nor the Saving of Japan would change as a result of currency exchange.

Myth 1.2: China should use its dollars to help its poor

Another related myth takes the view that China "should" use a big block of its USD reserves "to improve health care and similar services for the poor in China." But that is really not possible—unless people are envisioning thousands of American medical practitioners coming from the U.S. to set up practice inside China. U.S. dollars can be used only to invest in U.S. assets or to purchase goods and services from the U.S. (or to exchange with people from other countries who want to buy U.S. assets or goods). Dollars cannot be used to pay Chinese doctors or nurses or dentists inside China. If some Chinese doctors received dollars, there is nothing they could buy with the dollars. If the central bank permitted, they could exchange the dollars for renminbi; but that is not currently permitted, and even if it were, the end result would simply be that the Chinese government again owned all the dollars involved, and the doctors were just being paid by newly created domestic currency.

If the Chinese government wanted to use more of its dollar reserves to help the Chinese people, it could promote buying of more American medical equipment, American movies and TV shows, American aircraft, American construction equipment, and American-made clothes dryers. China could also trade some dollars in the market for another currency—euros, for example, to buy things from France, Germany, and Italy. Then the international investors who bought the dollars from China would own the USD assets, which they could use to buy U.S. goods and services when they want to. But the only way the dollars can ultimately be used is by purchasing things made in the USA or paying for services provided by Americans.

Myth 1.3: The U.S. is too dependent on foreign holders of Treasuries

Sometimes, we hear concerns that having a significant portion of U.S. Treasuries owned by foreigners puts the U.S. at risk if the foreign investors should decide to sell. But there is no need for Americans to worry about the proportion of Treasuries owned by foreigners. There are large amounts of international assets owned by Americans as well as U.S. assets owned by foreigners: while foreigners own nearly $23 trillion of American assets, including the international reserves that many countries hold in U.S. dollars, Americans own over $20 trillion of foreign assets.[5]

The U.S. has been running an international "current-account" deficit equal to about 3 percent to 4 percent of U.S. GDP. China, with a much larger population but a much smaller economy, has been running a current-account surplus of about 4 percent or 5 percent of its GDP. A number of other countries, including oil exporters, typically run larger surpluses as a percentage of their GDP, and often invest in USD assets: Saudi Arabia, Venezuela, Malaysia, Singapore, Switzerland, Germany, Norway, and the Netherlands all have had recent international surpluses of about 4 percent to 18 percent of GDP. Investors in a large number of countries own U.S. Treasuries, including about a dozen nations with more than $100 billion each.[6]

If many foreigners prefer the safety of U.S. Treasuries for their USD assets, that is fine for the U.S. financial system. If, instead, more of the dollars owned by foreigners were invested in U.S. corporate bonds or some other USD assets, then foreigners would pay Americans for the corporate bonds; the U.S. investors would then look for

[5] Source: Bureau of Economic Analysis, U.S. Department of Commerce. Figures are for year-end 2010.
[6] Source: U.S. Treasury Department.

someplace to invest those dollars, and in the end, more Treasuries would be owned by American investors. That too would be fine.

Of course, if any investors decided to sell a large amount of a particular kind of asset in a short time, it would put temporary upward influence on interest rates for that security. But the U.S. financial system is extremely large, with many assets that are very actively traded, and U.S. markets can adjust quickly: the U.S. Treasury market is especially huge and deep, far more than any other instrument in the world, with more than $500 billion traded *per day*. Even the largest foreign holders of Treasuries own only a few days' worth of such trading levels. Whenever holders of Treasuries sell some of those securities, they receive dollars that have to be invested somewhere in the USD financial system. As noted earlier in this chapter, when a foreigner buys or sells U.S. dollars, that cannot change the total amount of dollars in the system. Every day, some investors are selling some of the lowest-risk USD assets (Treasuries) and buying higher-risk dollar assets, while other investors are selling higher-risk assets and buying low-risk assets, notably Treasuries. In the open financial system of the U.S., different investors continually vary allocations to various dollar assets, in light of changing risk/reward views of the market.

Myth 1.4: America pays its bills by borrowing from abroad

We often hear that the U.S. has to "borrow" the money from abroad in order to pay for imports—to finance Americans' purchase of foreign-made goods. That is a concept which has applied historically to developing countries that needed to raise U.S. dollars in order to support their imports, but it does not apply at all to the U.S., where dollars are the nation's own currency. Consider an example of large-scale imports by Wal-Mart, from producers in China. Does anyone really think that Wal-Mart has to borrow dollars from China in order to pay for its purchases? Wal-Mart already has billions of dollars of cash on hand; if it ever wants to borrow dollars, there are plenty of banks in the U.S. that would be glad to compete for the lending business. Wal-Mart simply instructs its bank in the U.S. to deduct dollars from the Wal-Mart checking account and credit them to the U.S. bank accounts of the selling producers. Then the Chinese companies have to exchange the USD for yuan; the dollars go to an account in the name of an arm of the central bank of China ("People's Bank of China" or "PBOC" or "PBC"), and we are back to the situation described at the beginning of this chapter: China is looking to find places to invest the dollars, in USD assets.

As can be seen in all of the explanations behind these related myths, the U.S. does not "need" any foreign country to invest in U.S. Treasury securities. Treasuries are issued into the broad U.S. dollar financial system, which includes all dollars. The dollars that are owned by foreigners are still part of the U.S. financial system. If the foreigners choose to invest some of those dollars in U.S. dollar financial assets other than Treasuries, that's fine; but the foreigners will have to buy the other USD assets from current investors in the U.S. financial system. Those investors will then have the dollars, which have to be invested in USD assets, and some of those other investors will buy the Treasuries. The USD financial system always balances in total every day, and Treasury securities always have a home someplace in the U.S. financial system.

Comment: A different set of questions revolves around whether the U.S. trade deficit is too large a percentage of GDP, and whether foreign claims on future U.S. production are rising to potentially troubling levels—and what steps might be appropriate. Those are separate topics for legitimate analysis and debate. But regardless of the size of a domestic or international deficit or surplus, this myth, that Asian countries are bankrolling the U.S., and that America depends on them to provide money needed for the U.S. financial system, and to support Treasuries, is just not correct. This myth and the related myths are not only false, they seriously mislead a number of policymakers and interfere with international relations. The U.S. in a way does a great service for other countries, providing a very open, broad, and deep financial system that allows all owners of U.S. dollars an exceptional range of alternatives for how to invest the dollars that they might own, within the U.S. financial system.

Summary: Myth #1, "Asian countries are bankrolling the U.S., which depends on them to provide America with money and to support Treasuries," is **false**.

Countries that sell more goods and services to the U.S. than they buy from the U.S. end up with trade surpluses in U.S. dollars, which *must* be held in USD assets. There are only three things they can do with the dollars: buy American goods and services; invest in USD assets; or exchange dollars for another currency—in which case the new owner of the dollars will have choices one or two. All the dollars paid by Americans to companies, people, governments, or investors in other countries stay in the U.S. financial system.

Chapter 2

Myth #2

Treasuries "crowd out" financing for the private sector

Almost every day, we see articles in the press and in government statements about the effects of issuing Treasury securities to finance federal deficits. Many articles use the expression "national debt," and the same basic assumption: that when government issues Treasuries to finance a budget deficit, the funds available for the private sector are reduced, and thus productive investment is reduced. ("Crowding out" of financing is the term most commonly used.) Interestingly, this issue is not a matter of concern in China, which uses different methods of financing government projects, as described in Chapter 9. But experience in both the U.S. and China prompts serious questions about the presumptions underlying the statements, and leads to the need for examination and careful analysis of the premises, in light of how the financial system deals with and utilizes Treasury securities.

The Basic View of "Crowding Out"

The "funds crowding out" theory maintains that—with total private Saving at a fixed level—when government "uses" more money, private industry must use less. It's as if money is taken by the Treasury and then can't be used by a company that wants to build a new factory. The argument erroneously assumes that government issuance of Treasury securities must compete with corporate bond issuers for a fixed available source of investable funds, so that cash that might have been available for private investment is drawn out of the financial system by Treasury issuance, and that interest rates are thus broadly forced upward. But let's follow the money...

When the Treasury issues securities, it doesn't put the cash it receives in exchange under a big mattress in the basement of the Treasury building: the government distributes all the cash it borrows, so the cash goes back into the financial system. Money is not a consumed good; it is constantly recycled—unless the central bank removes some from the financial system.

While government *spending* (direct and indirect) on

goods and services could compete with private sector spending for real productive resources in a full-employment economy, that's a very different matter than using up "available funds" for investment. In the unusual circumstance of a full-employment economy, additional government deficit spending would likely put inflationary pressure on the economy; that is discussed more fully in Chapter 3.

Sometimes, the myth of "crowding out" seems to assume that, when the Treasury issues or redeems securities, it is changing the amount of money in the U.S. financial system. But in the U.S., only the Fed (the central bank), not the Treasury, can change the amount of money in the system. The Treasury, like private sector participants, moves cash from one owner to another. The Treasury can also increase or decrease the amount of Treasury securities held by the public, which are another form of government financial instrument; after such actions by the Treasury, the total amount of Treasury securities is changed, but not the total money held by the public. Treasury issuance or redemption also does not directly affect economic Saving—as explained in Chapter 3. Treasuries are critical tools in the balance of both the economic and financial systems.

Money in the financial system (other than the relatively modest amount used for transaction facilitation) seeks an interest-bearing home, by the close of every day. As new Treasury buying opportunities are introduced on the same day that the Treasury is sending money into the system, both the new Treasuries and the cash spent by the government find a happy balance: the cash placed into the system by government outlays finds an interest-bearing home in the newly issued Treasuries.

For many years, when the Fed put more cash into the banking system, a giant game of musical chairs occurred: no bank wanted to be the last one holding uninvested cash at the end of the day, which would have to be left at the Fed as "excess reserves." *Reserves* refer to commercial bank funds held at the Fed; *required reserves* are those needed by banks in order to meet the regulatory formulas based on their deposits; *excess reserves* are funds that the banks leave at the Fed beyond what are required. Any increases in excess reserves tended to put downward pressure on rates, as banks competed with one another by offering lower rates, trying to avoid being left with substantial excess reserves at the end of any day. Similarly, if the Fed withdrew money from the system, rates increased, as banks competed for scarce reserves to fulfill the required amounts. That approach was a very useful tool for the Fed for many years. But the situation changed dramatically during the recent financial crisis. Excess reserves held by banks at the Fed used to total about $2 billion for the entire U.S. banking system, so small changes by the Fed could have significant effects on the banks. In mid-2008, the financial crisis, combined with programs introduced by the Fed, led to very significant increases in excess reserves held by many banks. Now, in 2011, the total of excess reserves of U.S. banks is about *$1 trillion*. So, if the Fed adds or subtracts another $100 billion or so, it hardly has much influence over bank actions at the margin.

Individual Portfolios vs. the Financial System in Total

Often investors think about such issues in terms of their own individual portfolios, rather than the system as a whole. "If I had been reserving some funds in my portfolio for new investments, and I have just now used $100,000 of that reserve to buy Treasuries, then the money is gone, and I cannot invest that $100,000 in a corporate bond." But while that is true for that one investor, it misses the picture for the overall financial system. (This is a form of the "Fallacy of Composition," discussed more fully in Chapter 3.)

It's useful to think of the entire financial system in aggregate—as if it were one integrated bank serving the nation's financial functions. The system marvelously balances itself every day—with some help from the Fed, which, in its role as central bank, provides flexibility for timing differences, frictions, etc. In order for taxpayers to pay taxes to the Treasury and for investors to buy new

Treasuries, people, companies, and institutions withdraw money from their bank accounts and send it to the Treasury. That cash is used by the government mostly to pay its bills, to redeem maturing securities, to add to its Treasury account balances at the Fed, and, in rare times of a surplus, to retire some outstanding securities. As the Treasury receives checks from taxpayers and investors, it deposits the same total amount into the accounts of the people it is paying plus those whose Treasury securities it's retiring. The total amount of money the consolidated system "bank" has in deposits, its excess reserves at the Fed, and its ability to lend at the end of the day are unaffected by this exchange.

Illustration with New Treasury Issuance/Budget Deficit

Now let's use the analytic tool of thinking of the entire private sector financial system as an aggregate bank, to look inside the frequent case of the government running a deficit, and raising needed cash by issuing new Treasuries. Suppose Acme Corporation wants to borrow $100 million next week, and a set of investors plans to buy its bonds, using money in the consolidated system bank. In the meantime, the Treasury issues $100 million of its own notes, which are bought by other investors, using money they have in the consolidated bank. The myth would say that the funds are now not available for

Acme, since the purchase of the new Treasuries would drain the $100 million from the system. Then, says the myth, Acme would be unable to raise its funding, or would have to offer a higher interest rate, displacing some other private sector financing, thus reducing total investment in the economy by $100 million. That's not true, as we can see when we follow the money. Those dollars don't disappear. Money is never consumed—it only changes hands. As the Treasury takes in the $100 million of cash, the government distributes it to the public: by paying companies that provide goods and services for the government, for payments to individuals, etc. The recipients of those payments put that total of $100 million into their accounts in the aggregate bank. So, the same $100 million of cash is still there, in the banking system. It's true that $100 million of some investors' deposits has to be diverted to buy the new Treasuries. But then the deposits belonging to the recipients of the government spending (or others in the transaction chain) *replace* that $100 million.

By the time investors buy the Acme bonds, that $100 million may have changed hands a number of times, but it doesn't disappear from the financial system. There is no consolidated bank, of course, but the money behaves the same way. Instead of one entity lending and receiving the money, the distributed funds end up in many banks, but the result is the same: the money remains in the U.S. financial system, available for Acme to borrow. Dollars don't disappear.

The same concept actually applies in a somewhat different way with the private sector issuance of securities. If Acme issues $100 million of new bonds or shares, then some investors take $100 million out of their bank accounts and give it to Acme to pay for the bonds, and Acme puts that $100 million into its bank account. There is a $100 million increase in the amount of "risk assets" held by the public but no reduction in money. As Acme uses some of that money, it may get distributed into other bank accounts, but the $100 million always exists in bank accounts somewhere within the financial system. New bonds have been issued and are held in investors' portfolios, but there is no reduction in total cash in the financial system. For every buyer there must be a seller, and the money stays in the banking system, moving from the accounts of the buyers to those of the sellers.[1]

It's important to distinguish movements in interest rates from availability of funds. Interest rates might go up or down for a variety of reasons: because people perceive more or less credit risk or inflation risk, or because the Fed reduces or increases the money supply, or because there is more or less competition for real goods

---

[1] In fact, if a buyer is a bank, or if a bank lends some of the money used to purchase the bonds, the total amount of money in the system actually increases, as banks create money.

and services—but not because there are more or less Treasuries outstanding.[2] Interest rates on corporate notes and bonds might also change due to the risk/return preferences of investors.

But when the amount of Treasuries held by the public changes, there is no change in the aggregate equity and credit risk of the private sector. There is no reason why the aggregate total of potential investors and bankers, who were interested in taking on more credit or equity risk in exchange for higher expected returns, should have those views altered simply because cash has changed hands somewhere in the economy and more or less Treasuries are outstanding. The attraction of returns from providing money to businesses might change based on judgments about the economy, but Treasury issuance or retirement has *not* caused any shortage or surplus of "available cash." The purchase of the new Treasuries has not "crowded out" any private sector securities.

Reduction of Treasuries from a Budget Surplus

One aspect of the "crowding out" myth might be worded: *In the very rare times when the government runs a*

---

[2] There might be some change in the interest rate profile of the public, depending on the mix of Treasuries issued or retired. Theoretically, for example, if the Treasury issues a net new block of 10-year notes, that could tend to slightly raise 10-year rates, and lower short-term rates.

budget surplus and uses the excess cash to reduce out-standing Treasuries, more cash is introduced into the financial system, and the additional cash becomes newly available for private investment. Let's again follow the money...

As the public pays money to the Treasury (as taxes), the public receives that same amount of money back in another form (government redemption of Treasuries); there is *no* addition to cash in the financial system for investment in private sector securities.

Consider a case in which government cash flow is perfectly balanced, with no surplus or deficit. Then, a new tax of $100 million is levied, with the intention of reducing outstanding Treasuries by $100 million. In order to pay the extra tax, people have to use money they have in the bank; but at virtually the same time, the government puts the $100 million back into the private sector, in the form of payment to investors for redemption of bills or notes. The net effect on the pool of money in the private sector is *zero*. The same would be true if the surplus resulted from a new reduction in government spending. That $100 million would not be distributed for government payments, but instead would be used to redeem Treasuries from the public. The public as a whole would still have the same amount of money.

Either way, in a surplus or a deficit, the public gives the Treasury $100 million: by purchasing notes or by paying more in taxes. Either way, a segment of the public has to give the Treasury the $100 million that the government then passes on to another segment of the public, leaving the total cash held by the total public as it was the day before. Either way, the private sector has no more or no less cash available to invest. The $100 million may have moved around a number of times, but it cannot be "used up" or "consumed"; it must remain as part of the money supply, and the ability of the banking system to lend further is *not* affected by the issuance of Treasuries.

The Real Policy Issues

Running a budget deficit in a weak economy is generally helpful, because reduced taxes should induce increased consumption and production, or because the government will directly purchase production (such as road improvements) or distribute more cash to people who are out of work, and who are likely to spend more; but the deficit would not reduce the amount of cash in the system. The real long-term budget issue is **not** any reduction in funds available for private investment, it's the "structural deficit": whether in periods of full employment in the future, the government will likely have reasonable budget balance, or whether the combination of government outlays and tax revenues are likely to result in more total demand for goods and services than

the economy can meet at full capacity, leading to inflation. That is a question that deserves serious attention,
but is a very different matter from the false myth that
when Treasuries are issued, they "crowd out" other financing alternatives.

Summary: Myth #2, the assertion that "when the Treasury issues securities, they 'crowd out' other financing
activities, and when government deficits are reduced,
more financing becomes available for the private sector,"
is **false**. It is based on a misunderstanding of how the
financial system actually functions.

When the Treasury issues securities, it takes cash from
the investors and writes checks in an equal amount to
holders of maturing securities and to recipients of government payments. Cash moves from one part of the
public to another, and the public ends up holding the
same amount of money; there may be more or less in
Treasury notes outstanding, but the total money in the
system is unchanged, and there is no direct effect on real
Saving or Investment. The Treasury **cannot** increase or
decrease the funds available in the economy for private
investment.

Chapter 3

Myth #3

If everyone tries to save more, the nation will save more, and Investment, GDP, and employment will increase

We are often told that we should save more as a nation, and that GDP, employment, productive Investment, and thus future growth would increase if we all just saved more.

This myth sounds virtuous, and many in the media and government promote it. But, upon analysis, the myth turns out to be quite misleading, and it has had a particularly damaging impact on public policy, needlessly encumbering economic recovery. In contrast, Chapter 9 explains how China provides an excellent example of an economic program that has recognized the pitfalls of this myth and has done exceptionally well for many years with economic policies that defy this myth. Some distinguished economists have taken positions contrary to this myth, and this chapter has some commonality with some of those dissenting views; but the following exposition takes the analysis to further steps and conclusions that are very different from prevailing economic views on Saving, spending, and Investment.

No Nation Can Save Its Way From a Weak Economy to Healthy Growth

In starting to analyze this myth, it is helpful to keep in mind a concept known as the "Fallacy of Composition." It has a few versions, but the basic theme is that steps that might be helpful for a small number of people to follow may not be helpful, and may even be harmful, if a large number of people do the same. Consider a city where a large number of people drive to work every morning. Most people leave home at 8 A.M., and traffic is very heavy between 8 A.M. and 9 A.M. One person then decides to go into work early, leaving at 7 A.M., to drive during a period of light traffic. That might work very well for that individual. But if *everybody* decides to leave at 7 A.M., then the traffic jam would just move to the period of time from 7 A.M. to 8 A.M. It would end up not helping traffic overall. Nothing would be accomplished except to move the traffic jam from one hour to another hour, and require everyone to get up earlier.

There is a similar factor in economics, sometimes referred to as the "Paradox of Saving," or the "Paradox of Thrift": increasing Saving may be helpful for a particular family, but if *everyone* tries to save more, the total Saving of the nation *cannot* increase, and GDP and employment will decline. This paradox has been described in economics textbooks for many years, but the fallacy embedded in the myth seems to have been ignored or forgotten by many government officials in many Western countries. This chapter will explain how that applies to economies like the U.S., but first it is necessary to lay out some background and define some terms.

Some Key Terminology

In order to address this myth and others, it is helpful to clarify terminology regarding the main components of a nation's economy. For some readers, this will seem quite basic, but the basics are often neglected in analysis of big issues, and need to be defined clearly in order for further logic to proceed. Many public statements use terms in GDP equations without clear understanding of what they really mean. A fundamental concept that will be used repeatedly in these discussions is based on economists' representation of the key components of an economy. Consumption, Investment, and Saving are capitalized to indicate these terms' specific usage in the National Income and Product Accounts (NIPA) published by the Bureau of Economic Analysis (BEA) of the U.S. Commerce Department. The NIPA is the main source for data on economic movement in the U.S. For readers with further interest on this, more background is provided in an appendix attached at the end of Chapter 3.

The main GDP equation or identity is:

$$GDP = C + I + G + NEX$$

Gross Domestic Product, the total annual production of a nation, equals the sum of personal Consumption + Investment + Government consumption + Net Exports.

"Investment" is a very different concept than most people think of when they talk about their own personal investments. "Investment" in this context refers to private sector money spent on new equipment, buildings, houses, etc., which hopefully will have productive use in the future. This distinction is extremely important, and is often confused in public statements.

The BEA defines *economic* income and spending in special ways, reflecting their parts of the economy's production—ways that are only partially similar to more common uses of the terms. Chapter 7 explains more about the differences and explores some of the implications.

Personal Saving is then defined in a residual computation: the sum of all the people's personal *economic* income, after-tax, minus their economic expenditures. In this view of the economy, the portion of people's disposable economic income that they spend is called Consumption, and the portion that they do not spend is called economic personal Saving. This definition of Saving is very specialized, for a particular use in looking at economic production. It is very different from daily use of the term "saving," which generally refers to people putting money in bank savings account, mutual funds, and brokerage accounts. Economists generally love "Saving." Like everyone else, they also love "savings," their assets put away for future use, but what they really love is Saving, the deferral of Consumption. The basic rationale is that more Saving supposedly means more productive Investment, which should make future production more efficient. This chapter explores and challenges those assumptions.

The Chain of Transactions

Transactions in modern economies result in *sequences* of effects that need to be examined. Once we look at the chain of transactions, we can see that an increase in spending always has to generate a series of transactions that produce exactly as much Saving, so the net effect of increased Consumption on national Saving has to be zero: increased spending does not and *cannot* reduce national Saving.

Suppose a woman who typically saves $10 a week decides, this week, to go spend it: she wants to buy a cake from a local baker. The baker now has that $10, and he can either save it or spend it on something extra for himself as well. If he saves it, national Saving is unchanged: the woman saves $10 less while the baker saves $10 more. If he spends it on flowers, the florist now has the same choice. If she saves the money, total Saving is again unaffected. If she spends it, the choice keeps being passed on, until the total Saving is once again the same level at which it began.

This same chain of events also works for groups of people. If one group of Americans, used to saving $100 million a year, decides to spend it instead, the people they buy from now have that $100 million to save. This next group can also spend instead of saving, passing the choice on and on. In practice, people tend to save some and spend some. If the first group saves 33 cents of each dollar and spends 67 cents (sometimes called a "Marginal Propensity to Consume [MPC] of 2/3), 33 cents are immediately saved. Of the transferred 67 cents, the next group saves some and spends some, and so on, until the original amount of Saving is once again reached. Mathematically, the total Saving from such a chain has to add up to the original $100 million. The net effect of increased Consumption on national Saving is thus zero, and it has to be, as long as people are saving and spending some portion of their income.[1] However, we can see that GDP will increase as a result of the increased Consumption, and employment will increase by some amount in order to support the extra production for the increased spending.

"Wait," interjects a thoughtful reader, "is this book really saying that if people spend more, then national Saving will not decline?" *Yes*, exactly. Even though it may seem counter-intuitive, the logic shows it must be true. And there is more...

The Implications of Economic "Saving"

As noted above, the term "Saving" has a very special use in economics. A very key point—contrary to common myths—is that Saving does *not* provide the money for businesses to invest in a productive sense: for new buildings, equipment, etc. There is plenty of money already in the financial system of the U.S. to easily support far more than the current level of Investment—and, as

---

[1] On average, a small portion of consumer spending in the U.S. is spent on foreign goods. If some of the money in this chain is used for imports, then the exporters will be in the situation explained in Chapter 1: either they can buy more American goods, thus creating another step in the chain that maintains the Saving, or leave the money saved in the US financial system. Either way, the same total amount of money stays in the U.S. system.

explained later, banks actually create more money in the financial system as they lend to businesses for Investment purposes.

We often read comments by pundits and political leaders along the lines of: "To achieve our goals for growth, we need to raise the level of national Saving and channel those savings into Investment."[2] There is a common misconception that money has to be saved in a bank account or similar account in order to become available to support Investment, and that Investment cannot grow unless more of this Saving money that's put away is somehow then "channeled" to support the increased Investment. That is just a misunderstanding—one of a related set of common misconceptions.

But unless businesses want to invest more, no attempt at increasing Saving will work. If people try to save more in an atmosphere of slack Investment plans by business, it will just lead to less Consumption and less GDP in total, less Saving by the people whose income has been reduced, and no net change in total Saving. And businesses, of course, are unlikely to increase Investment when people are spending less.

Certainly some households and some companies need to shore up their balance sheets—reduce debt and lever-

---

[2] As will be explained, that concept is legitimately applicable only to conflicts of productive economic resources in a full-employment economy.

age—but that does not make it good policy for the nation as a whole. And that alone cannot produce economic growth: it may be that for those particular participants in the economy, reducing debt is key to preparing them for future spending, but only the spending can lead to more GDP. In the current economic environment, there are a number of individuals who do need to deal with excessive personal debt. Of course, many people cannot save more to reduce their debt, because they have no jobs. And the only way to increase jobs is to increase GDP, which requires that somebody spend more—on Consumption, on Investment, or on Government.

The Paradox of Saving really does apply. For a particular individual or company, it may be very sensible to try to save more. But for the nation as a whole, if everybody tries to save more, it will actually not result in any more Saving, but will just reduce GDP and employment. When people stop buying at the local coffee shop, the barista there loses her job. She then can't afford lunch at the local bakery, which in turn lays off another baker, and the chain continues.

Conversely, if Americans decide to *spend* an extra $100 billion next quarter, it will inevitably lead to a series of transactions such that the nation will have at least the same amount of Saving and Investment as before, but higher GDP and employment.

Investment Leads to Saving, Not the Reverse

We often read statements from U.S. and foreign pundits and officials saying, "America should save more, to increase Investment." That is a major misinterpretation of the economic processes.

We know that in the National Income accounts of the NIPA, Investment and Saving must be equal for any economic accounting period (aside from the international aspects). A very great deal is made of this, but just because two things occur simultaneously does not make it true that one causes the other. For example, we can observe that every time the thermometer shows a higher reading, the room feels warmer. But that does not mean that the rise in the number on the thermometer has caused the room to become warmer.

The traditional view that Saving leads to Investment is completely backward. Rather, businesses have to decide to increase Investment in order for the nation to have any increase in economic Saving, and market forces subsequently determine a new balance for the economy. Attempts to directly increase Investment by increasing national Saving (which means reducing Consumption and Government expenditures) cannot work. In the real economy, plans for Investment have to come first and, as implemented, will lead to the Saving that must equal the Investment in the National Income and Product Accounts.

As noted earlier, the NIPA computes Saving as a residual; income from all economic sources, including from production of Investment goods and services, is added up, then taxes and economic Consumption are subtracted, to reach figures for personal Saving. So, the computation of Saving is done on the basis of Investment production that has already occurred.

Let's look at the process by which Investment arises from business decisions, and can lead to a corresponding amount of Saving. Envision an economy at less than full employment in which most production is consumed; there is little Saving and Investment. Then, some entrepreneurial business decides it will build a new, efficient factory. It borrows $1 million from an enterprising bank (which can create most of the money). The Investment of $1 million gets paid to workers and companies, who have an overall marginal propensity to consume (MPC). That leads to a chain of spending and Saving, with money being passed from one person to the next as they spend, resulting in perhaps $1.5 million of new Consumption, and exactly $1 million of Saving. The $1 million of Saving equals the $1 million of Investment that was initiated by business. We know from the discussion earlier in this chapter that, whether the average MPC is high or low, and regardless of where in the chain of events one takes a measurement, the new spending on Investment will lead to an equivalent amount of Saving.

Another way to see how Investment creates Saving is through an example of an isolated farming community. Imagine three farmers who buy crops from one another, each trading $100. Total consumption and production (GDP) equals $300. The farmers are just growing crops that they trade with each other to consume; i.e., there is no Saving or Investment, as everyone works to produce goods for current Consumption.

Then one farmer devotes a year to building better equipment for all of them. The other two pay him $100 as an advance for the new tools. Total Consumption equals $200, Investment equals $100, and GDP still equals $300: the three farmers have produced just as much of value, but now some of it is equipment they can use to be more productive in the future. To do so, no one needed personal Saving or bank accounts. They simply shifted some production to Investment. NIPA accounting would just record $100 of Saving, equal to the amount of Investment.

The farmers could have chosen to try to increase personal Saving, but would that be wise? Suppose instead of initiating productive Investment, they each reduced spending by $50, buying only $50 of crops from each other. Total consumption and production then would be $150, instead of $300. They would produce less, GDP would fall, and no Investment would occur.

If they tried to continue to save more, the problem

would become worse, as GDP would drop even further. We've seen this spiral in action, starting with the drop in consumption of 2007. The Bureau of Economic Analysis would count the unsold crops as "inventory investment," and then inventory loss as they spoil. But there would be *no* additional real Investment in equipment. *Nothing* is accomplished; the attempt to create Saving would just reduce Consumption and actually create *no* productive Investment.

Perhaps the local bank might approach those who make the equipment for the community, and suggest that a loan might be made to them at relatively low interest rates so they could expand their equipment production. But why would they want to expand production of equipment (Investment) at a time when they could see demand declining? If anything, they would be more likely to want to *reduce* Investment in light of the declining GDP. That, of course, is what actually happened in the United States in 2008 and 2009, as Investment declined substantially despite very low interest rates. If businesses invest less, then GDP and income and Saving will all decline; the lower amount of national Saving will equal the lower amount of Investment. If businesses invest more, then GDP, income, and Saving will all increase, and the higher amount of total national Saving will equal the new higher level of Investment.

Economic Theory: Assumptions vs. Reality

One theory behind the misconceptions in the myth is that lower interest rates would automatically lead Investment to increase by an amount equal to the intended extra Saving. Economics students are often presented with models that *assume* constant full production, so that if Consumption falls, Investment is assumed to rise by the same amount. These perfect conditions suggest that as interest rates fall they will induce businesses to invest more. But real economies cannot be counted on to have such good automatic adjustment fortune. Clearly it was not so in recent years. The U.S. and a number of other countries have had periods (including recent years) with very low interest rates but with low levels of national Investment. Business managers know this is because they are reluctant to build new factories and equipment, at any interest cost, when they see sales lower with no sign of increase. Good modern economists know that businesses are not generally inclined to increase Investment when they see their customer demand decline.

It is true that, if an economy is already at full capacity, with full employment, then there can be conflict between resource demands for Consumption, Government, Investment, and Exports. In such a rare situation, if there were a reduction in some combination of Consumption, Government, and Net Exports, then there would be more room for Investment to grow, *if there were strong continuing business demand for more Investment.* In such a case, Saving would be increased, by definition, as a result of increased spending on Investment, displacing some spending on Consumption or Government. But this condition would be applicable only in a full-capacity economy, and it assumes underlying business demand for higher levels of Investment even in light of declines in other demand. It would clearly be inappropriate to apply an approach that might be helpful in a full-employment economy when, in fact, there is high unemployment. And, of course, there is always risk that artificial efforts to promote Saving and Investment could result in poor economic allocations; there is clearly evidence that some Investment turns out to be unproductive or excessive, as in the examples of real estate overbuilding in the U.S. and other countries.

GDP Growth Requires Spending

In order for the GDP of a nation to grow, someone has to spend more: on Consumption, on Investment, or on Government (or exported goods). People will debate the theoretical "best" balance of increased spending—between Consumption, Investment, Government projects, and Exports—but unless someone spends more on something, GDP cannot increase.

As experienced business executives know, cost management is very important, but it is not possible to build a business purely through cost reductions. It is necessary to also spend wisely for the future. If a business focuses solely or excessively on expense management, without sufficient attention to building customer spending on products and services, the business cannot grow. The same principle applies to a nation. Cost management by government and business can certainly help efficiency, and it is important for government to minimize unproductive interference in private sector activities, but in order for an economy to grow, someone has to increase spending of some sort.

China has dealt well with this issue—although there is much more to be done in the future, especially to develop the consumer sector. In light of the high propensity to save in China, the government has developed ways to generate more spending in order to build GDP growth. This success story is explained further in Chapter 9.

The Source of Funds for Economic Investment

But, someone will ask, doesn't the economy need Saving first, so that the bank will have the money to lend to business for them to make Investments in equipment? Well, No. Banks already have plenty of money to lend to businesses, even before the year's economic Saving is developed as a consequence of Investment. Banks have funds accumulated over time, plus funds from transaction accounts, in addition to savings accounts. Banks can also "create" deposits as they lend, as long as they have a modest amount of excess reserves at the Fed. Currently, U.S. banks have a huge amount of excess reserves by historical standards, and are able to grow loans by large amounts without requiring any new deposits.

Some might ask, "Doesn't corporate Saving result in business Investment in factories and equipment?" Again, the answer is quite contrary. Corporate Saving means that a company has earned more than it paid in dividends. But a company with Saving may or may not be Investing in new production. And, if Company A has Saving, that will certainly not force or even induce Company B to invest in new equipment. Again, it is Investment that leads to Saving. When national Investment declines, GDP falls, and many companies have lower profits and Saving. If Investment grows as a result of business seeing new opportunities, then GDP and national Saving will rise. There is absolutely no need for more "savings funds" in order to support further growth of productive Investment; what is needed is more of the combination of confidence, innovation, and development that leads businesses to decide to invest more for the future. If businesses do decide to invest more, there is no need for any "new savings funds"; there is more than enough money already available in the U.S. financial system.

It may be understandably difficult for some people to accept some of these concepts that differ so greatly from commonly stated views. To a large degree, the difficulty is the result of unfortunate choices of wording by economists many years ago, when they assigned names to portions of the economic National Income and Product Accounts. If they had chosen something like "Economic Income Residual" instead of "Saving", it would have avoided a lot of misconceptions. "Saving," as used in the NIPA, is just very different than in ordinary life. If they had chosen something like "Equipment and Building Expenditure" instead of "Investment," that would have helped, too, since "Investment" as used in the NIPA is very different from what most people understand it to be—investing in stocks or bonds or CDs. Once we clear our minds of the conventional implications of the terms, it becomes easier to follow the logic.

It becomes even clearer the more we think about it. The common interpretation is that, every year, people have to save enough money to provide the funds business need to build new equipment and facilities in that year. But what happened to all the money in the banks at the end of the prior year? Has all of the past money disappeared, or been "used up," leaving the economy to build new financing every year? Every quarter? Of course not. The term Saving is used in the NIPA in a different way. Saving has a specific relationship with Investment, because of how they are defined. But economic Saving is simply a residual computation, and in a given year has almost no bearing on or relationship to the amount of "savings" that people have in their banks and brokerage accounts, or that they add to those accounts, or to the amount of money available to fund business Investment projects.

Implications for Economic Policy

The economy will be best off if individual consumers spend what they can properly afford. For some, more saving is wise. For those who can afford to spend, it will help the economy if they do spend more; their increased spending will increase GDP and will *not* reduce national Saving.

It is good for an economy when businesses make productive investments, but the decisions in the U.S. are up to each business; government can help by minimizing undue overhead and excessive regulation, and generally supporting business growth and success. Business spending will *not* reduce national Saving. Business Investment will *increase* national Saving.

Growth in Net Exports would be helpful, and increased exports can be achieved, but it would be very difficult for that factor to fully compensate for declines in Consumption and Investment in the U.S. economy.

That leaves government with the key role to fill in when Consumption and Investment are insufficient to keep the economy at or near potential full-employment GDP. Tax reduction and/or spending increase by government in a slow economy will increase GDP and will *not* reduce national Saving. And some of the government spending can include development of infrastructure that can help future productivity. (Chapter 9 expands on China's great success in this regard.)

Summary: Myth #3, "If everyone spends less, the nation will save more, and GDP and employment will increase," is **false**.

It *cannot* be correct, analytically. The only way for GDP and employment to grow is if spending *increases* in the nation—spending by consumers, by business, by buyers of American exports, or by government. The terms "Saving" and "Investment" have very special meanings in the economic tables for GDP. "Saving" is a residual figure that means spending that is not for Consumption or Government; it does not refer to the sum of amounts put in banks or funds by people saving money in the ordinary sense of the word. And reducing spending cannot help the nation as a whole. If everyone tries to save more, then national Saving and Investment cannot increase, but GDP and employment will decline. If spending increases, national Saving will *not* be reduced. Investment leads to Saving, not the reverse. The financial system has plenty of money available to finance business Investment, independent of this year's economic Saving developed as a consequence of the Investment. *No nation can save its way from a weak economy to healthy growth.*

Appendix to Chapter 3
Some Perspectives on the GDP Equations

The capitalized terms Consumption, Investment, Government, and Saving are defined in very particular ways in the National Income and Product Accounts (NIPA) published by the Bureau of Economic Analysis (BEA) of the U.S. Commerce Dept.

The main GDP equation or identity is:

$$GDP = C + I + G + NEX$$

C – Consumption spending by consumers for goods and services has been running at about 70 percent of GDP in the U.S., and includes some very specialized elements, discussed in Chapter 7.

I – Investment is a very different concept than most people think of when they talk about their own personal investments. "Investment" in this context refers to private sector money spent on new equipment, buildings, houses, software, etc., that hopefully will have productive use in the future. This distinction is extremely important, and is often confused in public statements. For example, if you buy stock in Google or General Electric, or buy an existing house, that is *not* considered Investment for economic purposes; if, however, you build a new house, that *is* included in national Investment.

Economists generally consider Investment to be good, since it should lead to more productivity in the future— especially more production of consumer goods and services. (Investment actually can include inventory build-up, which is just accumulation of already made goods that cannot be sold currently; and sometimes Investment that looks like it will be productive turns out otherwise.) In some countries, including the U.S., government investment in buildings and roads is categorized as G, and is not included in this category.

G – Government expenditures for consumption (and, in the U.S., government investment in buildings) include the costs of employing people to help run the government and paying bills for services and production provided for government, including for law enforcement and defense. This figure in the U.S. generally has been about 20 percent of GDP: about 12 percent for state and local government, and about 8 percent of GDP for federal government, of which about 5 percent is defense. "G" excludes "transfer payments," which are payments made to other people, such as Medicare, Medicaid, Social Security, and unemployment benefits; but money spent by the recipients is counted as part of Consumption.

Transfer payments in recent years amounted to about 12 to 16 percent of GDP. Most of the expected growth in federal outlays, which receive much warranted attention, are in that category. Government consumption plus transfer payments have recently amounted to about 35 percent of GDP.

NEX – Net Exports equals exports to other countries minus imports from other countries. In recent years, this figure has been running at about *negative* 3 to 4 percent of GDP for the U.S.—negative since imports exceed exports.

S – Total Saving for the U.S. (as defined in the NIPA tables) equals total personal Saving plus corporate Saving plus "government Saving." Economists define personal Saving in a residual computation as the sum of all the people's personal *economic* income, after-tax, minus their economic expenditures. This definition of Saving is very specialized, for use in looking at economic production, and is very different from daily use of the term "saving," which generally refers to people putting money in bank savings accounts, mutual funds, and brokerage accounts. For example, in the NIPA definitions of personal Income and Saving capital gains are *not* included. (The reasons for that treatment have to do with the economy as a whole: if one person receives $100,000 for the sale of stock, someone else has to pay him, but nothing is produced; the S and I refer only to activities related to economic production of GDP. For more complicated reasons, the taxes that people pay on capital gains are deducted from after-tax income, even though the capital gain itself is not included in pretax income.) The Bureau of Economic Analysis explains that Saving is a "residual" computation; it is *not* computed from the totals of money that families save. These matters are further explored in the discussion of U.S. Saving figures in Chapter 7.

In the U.S., total bank deposits and currency (money) amount to about $10 trillion, while the total value of all assets, at current market prices, exceeds $100 trillion. People can use money to buy assets, such as stocks, bonds, and real estate. When one person buys a stock, money is transferred from the bank account of the buyer to the bank account of the seller; the total amount of money in the system is unchanged, even though the stock price may change.

Economic Saving is a different concept still. During the financial crisis in 2007-09, the value of total assets in the U.S. fell by nearly $20 trillion, so the accumulated savings or wealth of Americans dropped nearly 20 percent. But the money supply *increased* during that same period of time, while annual economic Saving dropped by about $700 billion, and personal income actually increased slightly, as explained in Chapter 7.

S has to be equal to I for any period of time in an economy (aside from international aspects). This is just an algebraic consequence of the particular definitions. Often people make the mistake of assuming that because S and I have to be equal, that S somehow *causes* I, which is a concept that does not reflect the real world. Before the international dimension is introduced, the fact that S = I simply means that S, which represents all of the economic activity that is not devoted to consumption or government services, has to be equal to the economic activity of production equipment and buildings, called I, since total GDP equals C + G +I. (When international trade is introduced into the picture, the equations become GDP = C + G + I + NEX and S = I+ NEX.[3])

---

[3]This means that, for a net exporting country, amounts of economic activity not spent on Consumption or domestic productive Investment or Government services go toward producing goods for other countries. For a net importing country like the U.S., NEX is negative, and total domestic production is less than the total amount spent on C+ G + I. Total domestic Saving (economic activity not spent on C or G) equals I less net imports (production provided by other countries).

Chapter 4

Myth #4

If the deficit is reduced, then national Saving and Investment will increase

We are often told that when the government runs a deficit, then government is drawing national Saving away from the private sector and forcing reduction of productive Investment. And, we are told, if the government actually ran a surplus—where tax revenues exceeded expenditures—then the government "Saving" would add to national Saving and Investment. But in light of what we have seen in Chapters 2 and 3, can those statements really be right? Where does the government get the money it saves? Where does the money go?

We know, from the analysis in Chapter 3, that attempts to increase Saving cannot result in increased Investment, and that it is really business actions to increase Investment that lead to a rise in national Saving. This chapter takes some different approaches to delving into these points specifically with respect to what is called government Saving.

Note: This myth is not about whether particular amounts or types of government spending or tax rates are "good" or "bad." Changes in taxation set off chains of secondary effects on both Consumption and Investment—effects that are subject to great uncertainties, and differ substantially depending on whether the economy has spare capacity. Those issues are important subjects for policymakers. But this discussion is different; it is about a key aspect that can be analyzed quite clearly: the financing of the federal deficit by the issuance of Treasury securities, and its effects on national Saving and Investment.

Behind the Myth: The Illusion That "Government Saving" Can Create Investment

"Government Saving" is an odd and misleading expression. Government receives its cash in two basic ways: by receipt of taxes and fees from the public, and by people buying new Treasury securities. Either way, the money has to come from people's bank accounts. As noted in Chapter 2, when the government spends money, that cash does not then disappear; it is paid out, and goes to the U.S. bank accounts of individuals and companies. When government Saving increases from higher taxes, private disposable income has to be directly *decreased*. When government Saving decreases from lower taxes or increased government spending, disposable income is directly *increased*. In order to understand the direct consequences of such government actions, we need to examine how the public comes up with the money to pay increased taxes, and where the money goes when the public has more disposable income as a result of paying less in taxes.

Government Saving and private Saving are two sides of the same cash flow coin. If the government ever runs a surplus, it returns surplus cash raised by taxation to the private sector by retiring securities. People put the cash back into their bank accounts, replacing the reduction in cash from their personal Saving that occurred when they paid the tax. As we saw in Chapter 2, there is no change in the amount of money in the financial system. The government does not provide the cash for businesses that are investing in real productive assets. The view that attempts to raise government Saving would increase Investment is an illusion. Consumption, GDP, and employment might well decline as a result of higher taxes, but total Saving cannot increase unless business increases Investment, and total Saving cannot decline unless Investment declines.

Government can influence the overall market environment, but in a free-market economy, government cannot directly change the level of Saving or Investment. This is in stark contrast to China, where the government acts to increase Investment not by encouraging more Saving, but by directly initiating Investment, which also results in Saving (as we will see in Chapter 9).

Now let's examine the two branches of this myth: first, in the case of deficit reduction, and then in the case of a larger deficit.

The Common Belief That Reduction in the Deficit Would Increase National Saving and Investment

Many commentators believe that a reduction in the deficit, from either increased taxes or reduced government outlays, would add to national Saving and thus to Investment. This opinion is often applied to long periods of time, both slow and strong economic times. Let's follow the money and the chain of transactions to see inside this myth.

It will be helpful to look first at a simple, but rare, example in which government might actually generate a surplus during a year. Suppose the budget had been in balance, and then government raises personal taxes by $100 billion. This would be called "government Saving" (strictly speaking, the government account is less negative by $100 billion). But, as we know from earlier chapters, money is not consumed. Government takes money from people in the form of taxes and gives the budgetary surplus back to people in the form of cash to reduce outstanding Treasury securities. To pay their taxes, the public draws from their private sector financial assets and gives cash to the government; the government gives the cash back to the public in the form of Treasury retirement; and the public then places the cash back into private sector financial assets. This results in a net change of *zero* in private sector cash, and a net effect of *zero* on national Saving.

Another misconception is that an added consumption tax or VAT would produce more national Saving. But we can see from the flows of money that while it might well reduce Consumption, it could not increase national Saving, since personal Saving would decline by an amount equal to the increase in government Saving. As explained earlier, it would make no sense to try to deliberately reduce Consumption (except perhaps in the rare times of very strong, overheating economies). And it would be particularly perverse to try to lower Consumption during a time of high unemployment.

Now let's consider government spending reduction. Suppose government spending is reduced by $100 billion with no change in taxes, meaning the deficit is lowered by $100 billion. So, some people who previously received that $100 billion from the government, directly or indirectly as income, will now not receive it; aggregate disposable income declines by $100 billion, and so personal Saving declines by $100 billion. Of course, lower disposable personal Income would likely lead to less Consumption, but as explained in Chapter 3, the end result for total Saving is the same: zero net effect on national Saving from government efforts to change the deficit. Government Saving has risen by $100 billion, and Personal Saving has declined by $100 billion, for a net change in total Saving of *zero*.

So as we follow the money and the chain of transactions, we see that lowering the deficit *cannot* directly cause increases in national Saving and Investment.

The Common Belief That Lower Taxes or Increased Government Spending Would Reduce National Saving and Investment

We are often told that one consequence of reduced taxes or increased expenditures of any form would be reduced government Saving, thus reduced national Saving and reduced national Investment. But let's follow the money. There might be a greater deficit, but would that mean less national Saving? There are two situations to consider: the economy is operating at full capacity and overheating, or it is not.

If the economy were operating not only at full employment but with productive capacity strained and overheating, then a tax reduction or increase in outlays could cause an inflationary environment. We know there are important issues to consider when managing deficits and minimizing excess demand on resources during very strong economic times, but issuance of Treasuries in the current year, to support that year's deficit, is a very different matter.[1]

Suppose the government reduces taxes but not outlays this year, increasing the deficit by $100 billion. This would be called "government dis-Saving" or "negative Government Saving." Government receives less money from people in the form of taxes, and receives the same $100 billion from people in the form of purchase of new Treasury securities by the public. The private assets are first increased by $100 billion, as taxes are lowered, and then reduced by $100 billion, as people buy Treasuries, for a net change of zero in private-sector assets. Even though the expression "government dis-Saving" is used to describe this process, the steps do not involve government taking any more cash from the public as a whole, and do not mean taking cash from businesses that are investing in real productive assets; government merely takes in less cash from the public in the form of taxes and takes in more for Treasury securities. Total national Saving and Investment are not directly affected.

---

[1] Various commissions have emphasized a focus on the growth of costs of Medicare and Medicaid over time, as well as pension costs at the state and local levels.

Economists looking at Saving think in terms of real production. A similar logic applies when considering the implications on national Saving from a reduction in government spending. If, during a slow economy, government decided to decrease outlays by $100 billion, then that amount of economic activity would be reduced, and all the people and companies who were previously performing economic activities reliant upon that $100 billion would no longer have that income. As explained in Chapter 3, a block of such income always has a chain of transactions following it, and that chain always produces an amount of Saving equal to the initial spending. So, if government reduces spending by $100 billion, then there will be economic Saving of $100 billion in the government account, and a reduction of $100 billion in private Saving, for a net impact of zero on national economic Saving. Reductions in government outlays are appropriate to plan for strong economic times. But in a slow economy, reductions in government spending will result in lower GDP, lower personal Income, lower employment, and lower personal Saving, with no direct effect on total national Saving and Investment.

Heat and Air Conditioning

There is nothing "wrong" with deficits in a slow economy. Quite to the contrary, it would be irresponsible to try to balance the budget during slow economic times with high unemployment, just as it would be irresponsible not to plan for how to keep the primary budget reasonably balanced during strong times of low unemployment and high capacity utilization in the future. Heat is useful in the winter, air conditioning useful in the summer. Insisting on a single deficit-reduction policy applicable at all times would be like insisting that air-conditioning is always right and proper, even when the temperature falls to 20°F and heat is clearly needed.

During a recession a deficit is generally likely, as "automatic stabilizer" functions kick in—reduced taxes and increased income support for unemployed people are critical to keep the recession from dipping deeper. In addition, as explained further in Chapters 7, 8, and 9, additional stabilizing steps by government can be very helpful; such programs made a big difference in the U.S. in the latest recession and also helped China, which is not hampered by this myth, to avoid recession completely. Introduction of deficit "triggers," which would require spending reductions and/or tax increases during recessions, would be pro-cyclical and could lead to much more severe recessions.

Theory vs. Reality: "If it were possible..."

Some people who advocate the myths about "government Saving" may, more precisely, mean something along the lines of: "If it were possible to have an economy with more productive Investment (and thus more Saving), then that economy could grow more rapidly in the future through the use of the increased productive Investment and thus produce more usable goods and services over time."

That might be true in a theoretical model but would be extremely difficult to achieve, in reality, through government actions. *Unfortunately, in any case, a full employment economy arises infrequently.* Economic conditions of serious unemployment and excess capacity are far more common. Unemployment in the U.S., for instance, was below 5 percent in just six of the past 40 years.[2] Many other countries have had higher levels of unemployment in most years.

Secondary, Indirect Effects

Once we understand that government surpluses or deficits will not and cannot directly change total national Saving, the next questions have to do with secondary, indirect effects. While the direct effects can be determined conclusively, secondary effects, such as how consumer and entrepreneurial behavior might be influenced, are the subjects of various theories. Economics students are

---

[2] Source: Bureau of Labor Statistics.

often presented with models that assume constant full production, so that if Consumption falls, Investment is assumed to rise by the same amount. Real economies cannot be counted on to have such good fortune.

It is helpful in this process to keep in mind that, in the National Income accounts, personal Saving really means not consuming. Each time that we consider a claim that any attempt to increase personal Saving can increase Investment, it is helpful to replace "increase Saving" with "reduce Consumption."

One theory is that lower interest rates would lead Investment to rise after a tax increase, by an amount equal to the government Saving. But, as noted in Chapter 3, while changes in interest rates are one of the factors that influence business Investment decisions, they are a secondary factor. Businesses invest to satisfy anticipated consumer demand (including for new and improved products), as well as to implement more cost-effective production. In the face of falling demand, most businesses *reduce* intentional Investment, even with interest rates falling; that was clearly evident in the recession of 2007-09, when interest rates were reduced dramatically, but still business investment dropped substantially.

It is true that an economy that has a reasonably balanced budget in times of full employment will be more conducive to noninflationary economic growth. It's also true that if we could maintain the same level of full-employment GDP with less Consumption, and if—despite that lower consumer demand—there were still more Investment, and if that Investment were productive, then the nation would develop the capacity for further growth in the future. But those are lots of ifs.

The principal concern about future deficits should be rising inflation during periods of full employment, and likely overheating, if the combined intentions for spending by consumers, businesses, government (and net exports) exceed the productive capacity of the economy. The way to avoid or at least minimize that potential inflationary situation is to reduce the planned future government deficit in times of full-employment (the "structural primary deficit").

Summary: Myth #4, "If the government reduces the deficit, then national Saving and Investment will increase," a.k.a the illusion of "government Saving" and Investment, **cannot be true**.

The notions that "government Saving" could *cause* business Investment, that lower deficits and higher taxes could *cause* more Investment, is highly misleading, and interferes with good policy.

"Government Saving" exchanges money between various members of the public but does not directly affect the aggregate Saving of the nation. Increases or decreases in taxes or government outlays affect private Saving in an offsetting amount exactly equal to the change in government Saving, thus leaving *zero* net effect on total national Saving.

There are good reasons for serious planning and actions to reduce structural deficits over the long-term, to be ready for full-employment years in the future. But this myth is not one of those reasons, and certainly cannot justify raising taxes or shrinking government budgets trying to reduce deficits during periods of high unemployment. Attempts to directly increase national Saving and Investment by increasing "government Saving" *cannot* work, and deficits incurred during periods of high unemployment will not reduce national Saving or Investment.

Chapter 5

Myth #5

Deficits create great burdens of repayment and taxes for our children

There are good reasons for concern about the levels of taxes that may be needed in future years, but there is an important distinction to be made between deficits that may arise during any future periods when the economy is operating at full capacity and potentially overheating, contrasted with deficits incurred in the past and currently, during a time of high unemployment. The myth states that deficits create great burdens of repayment and taxes for our children, from Treasuries now outstanding, and this year's new issuance causes more tax burdens for the future. That view reflects misunderstanding and misses the really important question, which is about potential tax burdens to support expenditures during *future* strong years. This chapter first summarizes the real issue, clarifying the potential problems in future years that may result from deficits at times of full employment and full capacity. Then, the discussion proceeds to explain why the myth, when applied to current Treasuries and deficits, is not valid.

Real Potential Tax Burdens for the Future

The principal concern about future deficits, as noted in Chapters 3 and 4, is that, during periods of full employment, if the combined intentions for spending by consumers, businesses, government (and net exports) exceed the productive capacity of the economy, then there will be inflationary pressure. If the costs in those future years have not been contained, then higher taxes would be needed to control the deficit and reduce the inflationary pressure. Much has been written about ideas for reducing the deficits of 2020 and beyond, and various commissions have produced good suggestions for legislation.[1] This analysis will certainly not try to duplicate those efforts; this chapter focuses instead on the myth of the burden of "debt". But often, public statements con-

---

[1] The biggest driving factors that need to be addressed are generally reported to be the costs of "entitlements" as the nation's demographics change. Some relatively modest adjustments to Social Security might deal with its impact, while Medicare seems to be a growing and complex challenge that could drive deficits in future years of strong employment.

fuse the potential challenges in strong economic times of the future with comments about the existing Treasuries held by the public, and with deficits incurred during periods of high unemployment, such as in 2011. The remainder of this chapter clarifies that distinction.

A Different Matter: The Myth About Taxes to Pay down "Debt"

We often hear public statements about how "irresponsible" it is for us to incur deficits in the present, issuing Treasuries that will become "great burdens to future generations of Americans." This concern was voiced repeatedly in the great debate of 2011 regarding the "debt limit." That legislative limit is actually computed using not only the amount of Treasuries held by the public, but also what are really just accounting entries for Social Security and other government "trust funds." These "funds," totaling about $4.5 trillion, do not really hold any money—there has never been any cash in them. They are totally accounting entries, made according to formulas, inside the books of the federal government. Although publications by the Congressional Budget Office make it clear that they understand the distinction, the historical tradition of computing the limit using "gross federal debt" for this legislative purpose prevails. The much more relevant questions relate to the real Treasury securities outstanding, sometimes referred to as "debt held by the public."

How could repayment of these Treasuries become a tax burden? Only if we believe that the total of Treasuries outstanding needs to be paid down some day: that the total $9.7 trillion of Treasuries held by the public has to be reduced to zero, or to some small figure, through increased taxes over time. But the U.S. has had Treasury securities outstanding every year since 1791, and has *never* paid down the total outstanding.[2]

Let's consider this myth in three ways: first, by defining the underlying interpretations and presumptions; second, by viewing the issue in the context of U.S. history; and third, by analyzing the nature and role of Treasury securities in the U.S. financial system and in its economic development.

Misunderstandings and Preconceptions

People often have misconceptions of Treasuries because they think of them as similar to personal debt. In many ways, applying the term "debt" to Treasury securities leads to a number of assumptions that are relevant for individual debt but are simply not applicable to Treasury securities. A number of people seem to be under the impression that, once the government has issued Treasuries to finance a deficit, then taxes in the future would have to be raised enough to "pay back" the money some-

---

[2] Source for data: U.S. Treasury Department.

day. That concept may make sense for an individual or a family: people may feel that, if they have personal debt, they would like to have it fully paid back before they die, so that their children will not have to worry about paying back the debt. The implication is that government will have to increase taxes on the next generation in order to "pay back" the "debt" incurred by this generation. Even worse, Treasuries are often maligned as inherently "bad" in "moral" tones, similar to a person with a gambling problem who incurs debt far beyond his means. Treasuries are inappropriately associated with an irresponsible government that cannot earn enough to pay the bills, so has to borrow, and may "go broke." But none of these concepts are applicable to U.S. Treasuries. While individual Treasury securities are redeemed at maturity, the aggregate total is never paid off, and there is no need for extra taxes to pay them down. U.S. government deficits, financed by the very special form of security called Treasuries, never are "fully paid back"—they never have been "paid back" in total and never have to be "paid back" in total.

Some Historical Context

The U.S. has a very long experience with Treasuries, with securities outstanding every year since 1791—and that has certainly not prevented America from great progress since then. Treasuries held by the public have never been fully paid down at any time.[3] During the last 50 years, Treasuries held by the public increased every year except for small reductions in five years.[4] The U.S. has gone through good times and difficult times, and met a great range of challenges, without ever suffering from some form of great "burden" from Treasury securities.

This country emerged from the Great Depression with massive government spending, which involved a deficit financed by issuing unprecedented amounts of Treasuries. The government started the 1930s very wary about issuing Treasuries, and gradually learned that they were essential to recovery. World War II then became the major force behind government spending, and the issuance of Treasuries made it possible for the economy to pick up so dramatically. Government outlays rose from about $15 billion in 1939 to $93 billion in 1945, while total GDP rose from $92 billion in 1939 to $223 billion in 1945. Treasuries outstanding increased more than six fold, and as a percentage of GDP, rose from less than 50 percent to more than 100 per cent. The deficit in 1943 was about 30 percent of GDP.

During that same time, unemployment fell from 17 percent to 2 percent. And, during that same time, con-

---

[3] In 1836, the total outstanding got close to zero, but not quite there. Since then, over the past 173 years, it has not even been close.

[4] Source: U.S. Treasury Department.

sumer goods and services also increased, despite the huge war effort, as the economy was productive in many ways: personal consumption rose from about $67 billion in 1939 to $120 billion in 1945; the U.S. was able to produce dramatically more "guns and butter." The economy went on to be very successful in the 1950s. The total amount of Treasuries outstanding fell slightly after the war, but the vast majority of the total amount stayed outstanding indefinitely. During that time, the ratio of total Treasuries outstanding fell as a percentage of GDP, since the economy was growing relatively rapidly for a number of years, but there was no program of increased taxes to reduce the aggregate amount of Treasuries.

Looking back further, Treasuries increased by a substantial percentage in 1839, but they were not a great burden on the next generation in 1869: the economy was doing fine. Similarly, Treasuries increased in 1933, but were not a great burden to America in 1963: the economy was in the midst of a strong period of solid growth. Treasuries increased in 1965, but were not a great burden to America in 1995, another time of solid growth. There is no reason to worry that Treasuries issued in 2011 will be a great burden to Americans in 2041. Quite to the contrary, Treasuries have proved extremely useful instruments over the course of American history.

The Role of Treasuries in the Financial System

The government issues various kinds of financial instruments, including what we ordinarily think of as
"money." Treasuries, paper money, government checks,
and reserves at the Fed are all financial instruments of
the U.S. government. The government, people, and institutions are constantly exchanging Treasury securities for
money classified as M1 (mostly bank checking deposits),
and exchanging M1 for Treasury securities. Economists
compute the size of the total amount of Treasuries held
by the public, as a percentage of GDP, just as they compute the various measures of money supply, but that does
not mean there is ever any need to "repay" money to the
Fed, or any need to ever fully "repay" Treasuries down to
zero. There is no good reason to use the term "debt" at
all for Treasury securities. That leaves us free to explore
the real nature of Treasuries, without the preconceptions
of "debt" as most people think of it in a personal sense.

Treasury securities, issued by the U.S. government, play
a unique and essential role in the financial/monetary system. The concept of interest-bearing components of the
monetary system is certainly not new. In the U.S., M1 is
defined to include currency and checking, and M2 adds
savings accounts and money market funds. The Fed also
has used a measure called "L," which includes short-term
Treasuries. Money in most modern countries, including

the U.S., is "fiat money," meaning that there is no specific asset (like gold) behind it. Money is an instrument of value: some issued and honored by the government, and some created by banks. A portion of money is readily usable in commerce to make payments, but some of it is not—savings accounts, for example, need to be converted to another form before they can be used for payment purposes. Banks have deposits at the Fed ("reserves"), which are guaranteed by an arm of the U.S. government (the Fed), but most deposits at commercial banks have only limited guarantees. All Treasuries are guaranteed by "the full faith and credit" of the U.S. government.

Treasury notes in aggregate are essentially equivalent to rolling, perpetual, tradable instruments with interest paid in kind. There are in essence sets of perpetual Treasury securities with varying interest computations. Some Treasuries have their rates based on prevailing rates for three months, and the rates reset every three months. Others have rates based on market rates for one year or five years, then reset to the then-applicable rates every one year or five years. All are fully tradable. This program has functioned very effectively for hundreds of years, with never any need to "pay off" the aggregate.

In many ways, Treasury securities play a role more like a form of "capital" that a corporation would use to help support growth. Many growing and successful corporations have ever-increasing amounts of bonds, rolled over but never repaid in aggregate. A number of corporations around the world have issued perpetual preferred stock, and view preferred stock and regularly reissued bonds as key parts of their capital structures. Some investors turn over their holdings from time to time, realizing cash, and other investors become the new holders of the securities. But the company never needs to pay down the securities in aggregate; it does have to pay the dividend or interest each year, but that amounts to only a small percentage of income, and can be paid in the form of addition to the outstanding perpetual securities, rather than in cash. Corporations consider such securities not as burdens of debt, but rather as a form of capital that allows the companies to build more for the future.

Recognizing Treasuries as a unique and critical component of the financial system helps to get over some of the stumbling blocks that arise from associating them with personal debt and all its personal obligations.

The government raises cash from the public in two ways: taxes and issuance of Treasuries. When the government taxes, people use their assets to pay the tax. When government issues Treasuries, it finances the needs of government and gives the people valuable assets in exchange. In fact, as highlighted in earlier chapters, periods of government deficits are parts of the economic realities, and the issuance of Treasuries is a key tool for dealing with economic cycles.

As noted above, Treasuries outstanding in total have *never* been repaid in full and are rarely even reduced. Normally, when Treasury securities mature, new Treasury securities are issued at the same time. So, although an individual security is redeemed with another instrument called "money," the aggregate of Treasuries held by the public is never eliminated. Occasionally, during rare periods of government budget surplus, some reduction is made in the total of Treasury securities outstanding. But the far more normal circumstance is to have a growing amount of Treasuries outstanding every year.

What about interest paid on the Treasuries? For many years, economists have distinguished between the total deficit of a government and its "primary deficit," which refers to the budget deficit excluding payment of interest on Treasuries. Interest on Treasuries is a small percentage of U.S. GDP; the key question is: what are the implications? If the economy is running with substantial unemployment, then it is better for the government to issue more Treasuries to pay for its needs rather than raise taxes. That includes paying interest on existing Treasuries by issuing new Treasuries. In the U.S. system that is done for some Treasury securities through a method of selling at a "discount," so that interest is incorporated into the face value, and in other cases by the mechanism of paying interest in cash, and then raising the same amount of cash through the issue of Treasuries. In aggregate, that is equivalent to the Treasury converting every million dollars of principal due for maturing Treasuries, and recording them on the Treasury books as $1.01 million (assuming 1 percent interest due). There is no additional cash, on a net basis, and no need for additional taxes.

In the rare cases when the economy is at full employment and overheating, then the government might pay interest in the form of new Treasuries, or the strong economy might produce enough government revenue to pay interest in cash. Would it make much difference in the overall economy? Not likely. Interest paid by the Treasury is income to the public holders of Treasuries, who have financial assets and are often trying to build wealth, rather than spending most of it in the year it was earned.[5] In a very strong economy, the government could well run an overall budgetary surplus, as it did in 1999. So, in a weak economy, the payment of interest by issuance of Treasuries could be somewhat helpful, while in a very strong economy, the interest would not be a significant factor overall, and total Treasuries outstanding might actually be reduced.

America is Not in the Eurozone

A number of commentators have raised questions

---

[5] The Federal Reserve has estimated the "wealth effect"—the likely increase in spending resulting from an increase in wealth—at about 3 to 10 percent of the increase in wealth.

about the ability of some eurozone countries to handle interest payments over time that have leached into the discussion of U.S. Treasuries. The concern is that, even if the structural primary deficit could be eliminated during a good economy, interest payments might continually lead to higher interest relative to GDP. Mathematically, such a problem could arise if real GDP growth were especially small relative to the real cost of interest on government securities[6]—but it is specific to eurozone countries. Treasuries have a very different balancing function in the U.S. financial system. (This important distinction, including why real interest rates for some eurozone countries can be very high, is explained in Chapter 6.)

In the U.S., GDP growth over long periods of time has averaged well above the real interest rates for Treasuries. At the time of writing, the U.S. economy was growing at a real annual rate estimated to be about 2 percent, while three-month Treasuries have a nominal interest rate of less than 15 basis points, with five-year Treasuries yielding about 1.5 percent nominally, and of course much less in terms of real (inflation-adjusted) rates. The real cost of Treasury interest continues well below the growth rate of GDP—with current real costs of interest to the Treasury actually negative, since inflation has

---

[6]After a year, the new ratio of Treasuries to GDP = starting ratio * [1 + (1-tax rate) * (inflation + real Treasury interest rate)]/(1 + inflation + real GDP growth rate)

been running about 2 to 3 percent.

There is another extremely important factor at the heart of the overall role of Treasuries: the U.S. financial system, including Treasuries, is always in balance, regardless of the amount of Treasuries held by the public. Investors receiving U.S. dollars for maturing Treasuries must put the dollars in the U.S. financial system; they could either buy new Treasuries or leave the cash in U.S. bank deposits (largely not guaranteed); if investors use the cash to buy another U.S. dollar asset, that would leave the seller of that asset with the same two alternatives. Chapter 6 explains this balance more fully: unlike euros, which can be invested in any eurozone country, U.S. dollars are always invested in the U.S. financial system.

Value-Added

There are some potential indirect economic aspects of deficit financing that are complex and difficult to quantify. The overall value of assets in a nation is related to future production and utility[7]; if there were new claims introduced, without sufficiently offsetting future increases in production or other value, then the real value of existing net assets should decline. But as long as the level of production is increased, or asset values are oth-

---

[7] The total size of assets in the U.S. is extremely large—over $100 trillion. Source: Federal Reserve.

erwise increased sufficiently, then the real value of existing claims should increase.

Funds from issuance of Treasuries can produce a wide range of added value as a result of government support for the economy, especially in slow times. Increased GDP and increased employment should help the overall value of a range of existing assets; improved profits from increased sales should raise the value of stocks in the market. And deficit spending used for development of infrastructure should improve the future productivity of the nation, which should increase overall asset values over time. In some other countries, as explained in Chapter 3, such infrastructure improvement is classified as Investment, rather than Government spending. Chapter 9 offers some observations about the economy of China, including its very successful use of infrastructure development financed through various means other than taxes. In any case, there is no burden of increased taxes on future generations in America to pay down Treasuries.

No Budgeting to Pay Down "Debt"

Although there are often comments about "the great burden" of past and current deficits, the people responsible for budget preparation do not actually plan for a process of "repayment" of outstanding Treasuries. In all the debates about the federal budget plans over the coming years, there has been, appropriately, a great deal of focus on how to reduce the annual deficit and someday be able to balance the primary structural budget, in years of full employment; and there is focus, inappropriately, on the cumulative budget over 10 years; but never any serious attention to a proposal for raising taxes/reducing expenditures enough to create a surplus sufficient to "pay back" the $9.7 trillion of Treasuries currently held by the public. Budget planners simply do not plan for "paying back" the deficits and Treasury issuance of the past; they know that it is not necessary and will never happen.

Summary: There are really two distinct issues at play here, which are often intermixed, but have very different implications. The deficit is projected to be too big in future strong years of full employment, but it is too small today, when unemployment is high and much more attention to improvement of national infrastructure is needed for the future. Legitimate concerns that could lead to future tax burdens have been addressed at the start of this chapter. But the myth that "outstanding Treasuries along with new Treasuries to finance the current deficit create great burdens of tax for our children" is **false**. America does not need to worry about any great burden of outstanding Treasuries on future Americans; our children and grandchildren will *never* need to repay the aggregate amount, and may not even *ever* reduce the total outstanding in any year.

The U.S. has gone over 200 years without ever fully paying down total Treasuries held by the public. There is no need to worry about paying it down in the next generation or the next. There is no plan for the government to raise taxes to pay down Treasuries outstanding, and there is no reason to develop such a plan.

It is really not helpful to use the term "debt" when referring to Treasuries, since Treasuries issued by the government have *very* different characteristics from debt of households. Treasuries are important and very useful tools for a nation in its financial system and economic development.

The U.S. financial system, including Treasuries, is always in balance, regardless of the amount of Treasuries held by the public. Investors receiving U.S. dollars for maturing Treasuries must put the dollars in the U.S. financial system. As will be explained in Chapter 6, this is very different from securities issued by eurozone countries, where euros redeemed in one country can be reinvested in another country.

The most damaging aspect of this myth is that it leads people away from the really relevant issues of economic policy. There are important but very different questions about how to manage deficits, and thus minimize excess demand on resources *during very strong economic times in the future.* But issuance of Treasuries this year, to support a larger deficit this year, in an economy of high unemployment, will not cause great burdens for the future.

Chapter 6

Myth #6

If the U.S. does not get its fiscal deficit reduced soon, U.S. Treasuries will face the same problems as bonds of Greece and Ireland

hallenges to the financing of Greece have been prominent in the news for more than a year at the time of this writing. Increasingly, Europe and other parts of the financial world have become concerned that Ireland, Portugal, Spain, and Italy—and perhaps more eurozone countries—might encounter the same difficulties. The same concerns have bled into the discussion of the U.S. economy, with some people asserting that if the U.S. does not reduce its fiscal deficit soon, U.S. Treasuries will face the same problems as securities issued by countries like Greece and Ireland. Statements along this line seem to imply worries that the U.S. might not be able to roll over Treasuries as they mature nor raise new money in the market. This concern is understandable for some eurozone countries, where there are valid questions about their ability to issue new bonds as needed, but to apply this logic to the U.S. is highly misleading. This chapter examines some of the key financial system issues for eurozone countries, and explores why the same underlying structural financing issues would not be applicable in the United States.[1]

This is a *different* question from the need for changes in the U.S. to promote a reasonably balanced structural budget during future periods of strong economic activity. As noted in other chapters, that is an important objective, but not for the reason stated in this myth. This myth has arisen alongside questions of the *financing* ability of the Treasury, regardless of the level of economic activity or unemployment at the time. The essence of this myth is the assertion that regardless of whether new spending is warranted, there is real risk that the U.S. might have difficulties issuing new Treasuries.

We often see opinions about the "upper limit" of public "debt to GDP"; sometimes 70 percent is suggested, other times 100 percent, while even others might say 150

---

[1] There is a political aspect, in that Congress periodically needs to approve a "debt limit," which can be controversial. But despite debates from time to time, no responsible government should want to have even a delay in approval of continuing authority for the Treasury. This book focuses on economic, rather than political, issues.

percent. Sometimes the figures use securities held by the public, other times "gross debt," which includes intra-government accounting entries. But these figures do not have a fundamental compelling logic. Economists have not discovered a new law of the universe in their laboratories; the figures are just estimates, based on different opinions. There seems to be little cogent explanation of why some countries are able to operate regularly with relatively higher ratios—sometimes much higher than the limits stated by pundits.

The ratio of Treasuries held by the public to GDP is currently about 65 percent for the U.S. In comparison, the ratio for Japan is about 200 percent. Japan certainly has economic challenges, but during 2010, before the earthquake and tsunami, its GDP grew over 3 percent, it had no inflation, and unemployment was only about 5 percent. Despite all the fears about the 200 percent ratio, the economy of Japan performed in 2010 in a way that would be the envy of most of Europe, as well as America. Japan has been smoothly issuing increasing amounts of Japanese Government Bonds ("JGBs"), which are widely traded, and we still read of holders of Japanese yen turning to JGBs whenever there is a "flight to quality."

Overall, the use of such ratios as "debt-to-GDP" provides some general trend data, but very limited insight into the issue, and thus little basis for reaching a solid conclusion.[2] There are two basic problems with the myth that compares U.S. Treasuries to eurozone nations' bonds and gives excessive weight to the "debt-to-GDP" measure. First, the myth treats Treasuries as "debt," in other words as if they were personal debt, which is just not applicable to U.S. Treasuries (as explained in the previous chapter). Second, commentators often make reference to eurozone countries with financing problems; but, as explained below, those countries do not have their own monetary systems, and their situations are very different from the U.S.

The implication of this myth is that, at some point, especially as the "debt-to-GDP" ratio rises, investors will just no longer want to own U.S. Treasuries. In order to understand the issues, it is necessary to look inside the U.S. dollar system. All dollars have to go someplace in the U.S. system. An international investor can choose to own securities in various currencies, but—as explained in Chapter 1—even if some investors sell U.S. dollar assets, the dollars do not disappear, they merely change owners. As some investors use money to buy corporate bonds or gold, then the sellers of those assets will deposit the funds in their bank accounts. U.S. dollars invested by domestic and foreign owners always remain as

---

[2] Similar thoughts with respect to the U.K. have been noted: over history, that ratio in the U.K. was 150 to 200 percent at various times. A few thoughtful commentators in the U.K. have raised questions about the use of the ratio.

part of the U.S. financial system. As maturing Treasuries are redeemed, the dollars will be looking for a home; for dollars, there can never be a less risky place than in Treasuries.

Treasuries in the U.S. Financial System

The U.S. (in contrast to eurozone countries and to state governments in America) *does* have its own monetary system; Treasuries and the Federal Reserve Banks, which house or control much of the dollars in America, are instruments of the U.S. government.

As noted earlier, the government issues different kinds of instruments, including what we ordinarily think of as "money." Treasuries, paper money, government checks, reserves at the Fed...all are financial instruments of the U.S. government. A very large portion of U.S. dollar financial assets is priced with interest rates based on the risk-free rates of U.S. Treasuries. There are very good reasons for that.

In the process of Treasury issuance and redemption, the money involved changes hands but cannot leave the U.S. financial system. There is a well-established system of "primary dealers" and auctions. It would not be unusual for the Treasury to redeem $40 billion and issue $50 billion on a given day. There is a huge, deep market for Treasuries, with an average of over $500 billion *per day* traded. Newly issued Treasuries are mostly bought by primary dealers, who pay cash from their bank accounts early in the day or are advanced the cash by banks, and then deliver most of the securities to buyers by the end of the day; the buyers pay with money from their bank accounts, transferred to the bank accounts of the dealers. The Treasury distributes most of the proceeds that it receives to the bank accounts of investors redeeming that day, and to recipients of government payments. Often, the Treasury uses newly received cash to replenish its deposit accounts at the Fed and commercial banks, if it has already distributed the equivalent amount from those accounts; the cash at that point is already in bank accounts in the private sector. One investor or another has the cash, and some own the new Treasuries. At the end of the day, the same amount of money as the day before is in one bank account or another.

Where can the money go? As noted in Chapter 2, when the Treasury issues securities, it doesn't put its cash under a big mattress in the basement of the Treasury building. The government distributes all the cash it receives, so the cash goes back into the financial system. At essentially the same time that the Treasury issues $50 billion of securities, the government is distributing $50 billion to the public: by redeeming maturing Treasuries, paying companies that provide goods and services for the government, for payments to individuals, etc. Many investors simply "roll over" their Treasury securities, replacing maturing ones with newly issued ones, and taking just the interest. For example, perhaps $20 billion of the $50 billion issue might be in that category. The Treasury pays out the other $30 billion to individuals in fulfillment of obligations such as Social Security and Medicare, and to companies in payment of bills for goods and services that have been submitted to various government departments and agencies. At that instant, a set of participants in the U.S. financial system will have the extra $30 billion and will look to place those funds. This example follows the case in which the Treasury will first pay out funds that it has in deposits at the Fed, and then proceed with the issuance of securities to replenish those accounts. (Treasury has been generally keeping about $100 billion to $300 billion on deposit at the Fed— that is in addition to the hundreds of billions of other assets, including gold and silver, held by the Treasury.)

In the whole of the U.S. financial system, the only place to put the funds is into the new Treasuries that are being auctioned—or otherwise leave the funds in bank accounts. If some investors choose to buy other financial assets, then someone else—the sellers of those assets— will end up with the cash, and will be looking for a place to invest it. There are no other USD financial assets to invest the cash that are not already owned by someone. As explained in Chapter 2, dollars that might be invested in corporate bonds that day will be deducted from the bank accounts of the buyers and go into the accounts of the sellers of the bonds, with no net change in aggregate available cash. And the dollars cannot go to another country, as explained in Chapter 1; an individual investor can choose to invest some dollars in assets in another country, but then the foreigners who sold those assets would just own the same dollars in U.S. banks. A process similar to a giant game of musical chairs occurs, as noted in Chapter 2: no investor wants to be the last one left, at the end of the day, with excess cash that is not invested at all. Investors who have the extra $30 billion of cash in their bank accounts have, in the end, two choices: leaving the cash in bank deposits, which earn very little, if any, interest, and are not guaranteed by the government beyond $250,000[3]; or buying the new Treasuries, which pay interest and have the "full faith and credit" of the United States.

Markets very rationally go to Treasuries for safety. In 2008 and 2009, when markets worried about the safety of many banks, the U.S. government came to the rescue, guaranteeing deposits and even some bank bonds, backed by the strength of the U.S. Treasury. When Treasury invested money into banks, in order to make them safer, that cash came from investors who bought new

---

[3] Except for a temporary unlimited guarantee for certain non-interest accounts.

Treasury securities at a time when the investors were uneasy about the security of "money" deposited in major banks. Essentially, Treasuries were used to protect the U.S. banking system, and were safer than "money," which is largely a form of liability of commercial banks.

Money and Banks

Most of the money in the U.S. financial system (M2, which includes checking and savings accounts) was created by commercial banks, and is backed by the banks, not by the government; it is essentially "bank money." A relatively small portion of money (deposits in commercial banks) is guaranteed by the U.S. government. Treasury securities are fully backed by the U.S. government. The Treasury agrees to replace each Treasury bill with bank money at maturity; the investors in specific maturing Treasury securities will have their government-guaranteed investments replaced by bank money, which is not guaranteed. But in aggregate, as explained in Chapter 5, the full amount of Treasuries outstanding will never be replaced by bank money—the aggregate total will remain outstanding permanently, and investors who receive bank money periodically will have the opportunity to reinvest in government-guaranteed Treasuries.

Even if some of the investors as a whole did leave some of the extra cash in their bank accounts, then the banks could use that money to buy the new Treasury securities, and would be likely to buy if the interest rates on those securities are greater than the interest rate on excess reserves at the Fed. The banks essentially have a choice of leaving their own invested funds with one part of the federal government—the Fed, earning the rate that the Fed pays on excess reserves—or buying Treasuries, which are another form of obligation of the federal government. At the time of this writing, U.S. banks hold about $1 trillion of excess reserves at the Fed, far beyond required amounts. The Fed can always encourage the banks to buy Treasuries by lowering the interest rate that the Fed pays to the banks on excess reserves. Currently, short-term Treasury bills are yielding less than 15 basis points (15 one-hundredths of one percent). The Fed has set the rate it pays on excess reserves left by banks at the end of the day at 25 basis points. That means that banks can earn more interest just leaving the money overnight with the Fed, rather than investing in short-term Treasuries. The Fed could lower that rate to 5 basis points, or zero; in that case the banks would have a clear financial incentive to use more of their funds to buy Treasuries instead of leaving such large amounts with the Fed. New regulations regarding liquidity measures will require banks to hold more Treasuries in any case, which will not be a problem, since banks have large capacity to buy more Treasuries.

Banks could actually purchase a *very* large amount of Treasuries from the Treasury as new issues, as well as from the marketplace, because, as they buy Treasuries, banks essentially create money as they do when they make loans. If banks buy $100 billion of Treasuries from other investors or the Treasury, then the banks will credit the deposit accounts of the sellers with $100 billion. If banks buy newly issued Treasuries, the Treasury spends the money, and it ends up back in the banking system as deposits in the accounts of those who received the government payments. The banking system still has all its reserves held at the Fed, but now about $8 billion of the reserves would be allocated to "required" reserves, associated with the newly created deposits; the purchase of $100 billion of Treasuries uses only $8 billion of the trillion dollars of excess reserves. The only limitation on bank purchase of Treasuries is the amount of reserves required for new deposits. Since the excess reserves of U.S. banks stand at about $1 trillion, the banking system could buy, theoretically, over $10 trillion of Treasuries.[4] As a practical matter, of course, that is not possible, since that would exceed the total $9.7 trillion of Treasuries currently held by the public; the computation just illus-

---

[4] Reserve requirements in the U.S. vary from zero to 10 percent; 8 percent was used in this example.

trates that it is possible for the banking system to buy very large amounts of Treasuries without strain or need to raise more cash.

Fortress Fed

At the end of the sequence, there is another option, which is unlikely to ever be needed. If for some reason neither the investors nor the banks decided to buy all the new Treasuries, and the Fed chose not to use its tools to make the Treasuries more attractive to banks, then the Fed could buy some securities directly or indirectly from the Treasury, essentially using the excess reserves that are placed at the Federal Reserve Banks by the commercial banks. If, for example, there were $10 billion of Treasuries without a home as the end of the day approached, that would mean investors had left an extra $10 billion of deposits in their banks, and the banks were leaving that $10 billion in their excess reserve accounts at the Fed; the Fed could simply use that money to buy the last block of Treasuries directly from the Treasury.[5]

---

[5] Another backstop in many countries is privatization: for the government to sell or lease some of its holdings of assets, including property and facilities such as airports. In some countries, including China, government sales and leasing of land to raise funds is a well-established practice. There are sometimes controversies about local implementation of specific transactions, but the principle of government raising revenues from the sale and lease of land and land-rights is well established. Hong Kong has for many years maintained low tax rates and financed the rest of its budget through sales

We know that some commentators express great concerns about what they call Fed "monetization of debt" or "printing money." But the experience of both China and the U.S. provide bases for putting those concerns in perspective. The main concern seems to be that if the Fed buys Treasuries, it will increase the money supply and perhaps cause excessive growth in lending, higher interest rates, and inflation. But in China, the central bank is constantly providing new renminbi for the banking system as it converts foreign currency from net exports into RMB; the central bank regularly issues securities to the banks, and buys some of them back as it deems appropriate. It all works quite smoothly (more on this in Chapter 9). In the U.S., we have recent experience with what is called quantitative easing ("QE"), when the Fed has bought Treasuries and other securities on an unprecedented large-scale, not because it thought it was needed to support the Treasury market, but rather to encourage low interest rates and increased economic activity. After the two rounds of quantitative easing in the past few years, often called QE1 and QE2, interest rates continue to be very low and the actions have clearly not caused excessive lending. Quantitative easing does not purport to create new wealth or new assets for the financial sys-

---

of land, including new land created by fill-in at the harbor edge. It is not the custom in the U.S., except for special cases such as the telecommunications spectrum, but the government owns assets with value likely far in excess of the total amount of Treasuries.

tem: it simply exchanges one form of liquid assets held by the private sector (bank deposits) for another form of highly liquid assets (Treasuries). Since the banking system already has huge excess reserves, there is no cash constraint on banks' ability to grow loans; QE did not matter in that regard.

As a practical matter, this backstop option is unlikely to be needed, because at the end of the process investors have cash they want to invest, and they find it more rational to put extra cash in Treasuries rather than in banks. Furthermore, the Fed always has the option of changing the overnight rate on excess reserves to make it more attractive for banks to hold Treasuries rather than reserves. If the Treasury spends $100 billion from its account at the Fed, then investors will be looking for a place to keep those funds in U.S. dollar assets. The $100 billion flows through the system and at every moment is domiciled someplace in the U.S. financial system, in the accounts of private or professional investors, at U.S. banks. If any investors buy existing assets from other investors, then the sellers need to find new investments, but there are no new places to put the money except for newly issued Treasuries. So, when the Treasury issues new securities, they provide a place for the funds to be invested and the Treasury can replace the same amount of money in its account at the Fed. In any event, there are always enough U.S. dollars in the U.S. financial system to support all the Treasuries. The Treasury and the Fed do their fund management jobs very well, and Treasury securities always have a home someplace in the U.S. financial system. These statements apply regardless of the size of the federal deficit or the accumulated amount of Treasuries held by the public. There is no cause to fear that any auction of securities by the U.S. Treasury would ever fail to provide the necessary funds.

The Eurozone is Very Different

In many countries around the world, the overall process for the issuance of Treasury securities is similar to that in the U.S., but with much smaller, shallower markets. There are two important exceptions for other countries whereby major problems might develop. The first is when a government has borrowed in a currency that is not the currency that it uses in its own domestic activities (or when its domestic currency is linked or pegged to the currency of another country). That kind of situation has been behind a series of international financial crises over the years, as a number of foreign countries essentially borrowed in U.S. dollars and could not raise the dollars needed to repay. The second potential path to crisis is when a country has securities outstanding in a currency that is not fully its own (such as the euro) without having its own central bank. In that sense, eurozone countries are more analogous to state governments in the U.S., rather than the U.S. federal government. It is possible that a state or municipality in America could have serious problems in refunding some of its outstanding municipal bonds; there have been times when issuers of municipal bonds have asked for rescue from the federal government, but no state or municipality has its own central bank. Neither California nor Greece has its own financial/monetary system, but concern because some countries in the eurozone may face difficulties with their securities simply does not apply to U.S. Treasuries.

U.S. dollars have to go someplace in the U.S. financial system: there are no alternatives for holders of U.S. dollars, as the U.S. financial system is where U.S. dollars live. But investors in euro-denominated bonds of Greece or Ireland or any other specific country *do* have alternatives when those bonds mature. The euros have to be invested in the eurozone, but euros are not attached to any particular country. Euros received by an investor from a maturing bond in one country could be placed in a bond or bank in any other eurozone country that the investor believes is financially stronger. For example, when Greece redeems bonds, investors receiving those euros may decide to re-invest those euros in Germany or France, rather than in Greece. That situation presents a particular challenge for eurozone countries that simply is not applicable for U.S. Treasuries, since all U.S. dollars have to go someplace in the U.S. financial system.

In light of the attention given to such issues in a number of eurozone countries, it seems appropriate to add some further comment, utilizing some of the concepts discussed in this book. At this time, Greece, Ireland, and Portugal are all involved in programs trying to deal with these problems. In the context of issues discussed in this book, there are four fundamental challenges: first, to deal with the need for government financing in the markets in the near term; second, to develop a program for getting the structural primary deficit in balance over time; third, to make policy, legal, and economic changes that enable more efficiency and competiveness; and fourth, to deal with the need for deficit financing during recessionary periods.

The first, immediate challenge of debt financing is currently being addressed by eurozone members and by the European Central Bank. At the time of this writing, the question remained open as to whether some form of "restructuring" of the securities of some eurozone nations would be necessary. The second challenge, the structural deficit, is being partially addressed in the context of the first programs, with various programs attempting to reduce the deficit and increase efficiency in applicable eurozone countries, but is very difficult, and more ideas are warranted. This author and his son, Dan Newman, put forward one idea in a short article repeated here:

A modern-day Odysseus steers a hard course. Investors worry Greece will rock the eurozone as it sinks in a vortex of default, yet they also fear ramming the nation against the cold rock of austerity. Each day, Greece awaits rescue either from wealthy euro nations insisting on the sale of public assets or from a European Central Bank demanding further budget cuts.

The initial bailout plan has failed; Standard & Poor's downgraded Greek debt to the lowest ranking on earth. As the officers of the Greek voyage steer between drowning and riots, Spain, Portugal, and Ireland watch anxiously from a few lengths behind. Yet there is another route to steady the ship.

By adopting a new unit for state payments—call it a "Talent," from the Greek word for balance— Greece can assert both independence and prudence. Applied to all public salaries and internal government payments, the new unit moderates the Greek budget with precision, automatically adjusting payments according to revenue. When a given budget is balanced, a civil servant earning, say, 50,000 Talents collects an equal number of euros. But when Greece overspends by 10 percent, those same Talents supply a salary of only 45,000 euros. Citizens then share the costs and rewards of fiscal restraint.

Why do this rather than quit the euro, as Pimco, the world's leading investor in sovereign bonds, argues is necessary? Because Greece would lose the trade and capital advantages of a common currency, and Europe might stagnate as other nations jump ship. Spain borrows a staggering 23 percent of its budget, and Italy now spends as much on bond interest as it does on public education.

Austerity, the other course, is easier to pledge yet harder to maintain. Greece proposed further spending cuts and higher taxes, but given the resulting riots, other European nations must wonder if the reforms will hold. They have already raised the retirement age and increased tax rates, yet they still seek short-term relief through eurozone bonds, which its wealthier and more labor-efficient neighbors view as asking their workers to put wind in foreign sails.

This doesn't happen in America or any country with its own central bank, where public debt balances with benefits and assets for its citizens. When an American buys a Treasury bond, private saving in the U.S. rises by an amount equal to any increase in the deficit. When America repays Treasury bonds to foreigners, they use the dollars to invest in the U.S., or to buy our goods, or transfer them to someone who will; U.S. dollars are always invested in the U.S. financial system. But euros may be spent in nations other than Greece, and when Athens buys, Germany holds part of the bill.

Europe can break free of this mess with a domestic unit for public payments, a self-correcting system that requires no external scold. Bond payments must be kept in constant euros to attract investors, but all other state payments can be denominated in Talents. In Greece, where 75 percent of public spending goes to wages and benefits, this amounts to a salary scale that slides with fiscal health.

If Greek spending exceeds revenue by 20 percent, each Talent becomes valued at 0.8 euros, and 100 billion Talents in the budget becomes 80 billion euros that Greece pays to its workers and contractors; the budget returns to balance in euros. If the Greeks wish to keep Talents equal to euros, they may increase revenue or decrease spending, but no one requires them—or relies on them—to do so. Greeks may then approve any budget they wish any given year, without the risk of their nation, or Europe, drowning in debt.

European nations can then enjoy a common market regardless of the spending habits of their members. Private industries exporting from Greece may even choose to adopt the unit system to stay competitive, offering contracts at a given level of Talents to remain attractive abroad. And other eurozone countries that are facing similar problems may choose a parallel course.

Greece, like its seaside neighbors, needs a reliable way to cover its own costs. With a new unit for public payments, it can do so while retaining the advantages of the European common currency—a challenging course, to be sure, but better than a shipwreck.

Such an approach, utilizing in some fashion a currency-unit-equivalent for government transactions inside the country, as a real or "virtual" second currency to the euro in Greece, would have to be implemented over a period of time, but has the potential to address long-term deficits. The specifics would be quite complex of course; this article was intended to spur different ways of thinking about the challenges. This line of thinking would also incentivize millions of government employees and recipients of government payments to seek a balanced structural budget.

The third challenge may be the most difficult: it will likely take years to make and implement new policy and legal changes that promote more efficiency and competitiveness, thus enabling these economies to succeed on their own.

The fourth challenge, allowing for deficits during recessions in order to avoid them turning deeper, is compounded by the austerity measures implemented in association with dealing with challenges one and two. Inevitably, during recessionary or very slow economic times, deficits can arise in any economy, and may be essential to keep a mild recession from growing deeper. Every nation needs to be able to finance deficits at such times. The fundamental problem is that some countries in the eurozone will just not be as productive and efficient as others, but the role of national government, as described in Chapters 3, 4, and 7, is severely limited by the fact that those countries issue securities in a currency that is not their own. That leaves open the question of whether some eurozone nations might be better off returning to their own national currencies and central banks.

What Eurobonds Can Learn from U.S. Treasuries

The eurozone has been struggling with how to finance support for member nations that face problems raising money on their own. One possibility that has been actively discussed is issuance of some form of "Eurobonds." The proceeds of these Eurobonds could be allocated to member countries, based on a set of guidelines. For example, the allocations might provide for funding up to X percent of GDP for a country in recession with unemployment over Y percent, possibly with some relationships to GDP and population. Mechanisms would have to be developed to deal with the existing bonds of weaker nations, and there are a number of proposals being considered in which Eurobonds could play a key role.

The general vision is that the new Eurobonds would be guaranteed jointly and severally by all eurozone members, possibly issued through a special stabilization fund or some other mechanism that essentially relies on the creditworthiness of major eurozone members to support repayment. But there is a natural resistance to issuance of the Eurobonds from strong member countries, including Germany, whose citizens fear that they might have to pay increased taxes to support weaker countries, such as Greece. That issue has become a major challenge to the program.

There is another alternative, which can avoid that vexing problem: to structure Eurobonds modeled on U.S. Treasuries, as described in Chapters 5 and 6. As explained for U.S. Treasuries, there would be no need for any countries in the eurozone to worry about having to raise taxes in the future to pay off Eurobonds that support financially troubled member nations. The eurozone does not have a central treasury, but it does have a central bank; so, the Eurobonds could be issued by the European Central Bank (ECB), with its "full faith and credit"—equivalent to its issuance of euro currency. The

Eurobonds could be issued in forms similar to series of U.S. Treasuries, continually rolled over, and with a deep and highly liquid market developing.[6]

Eurobonds structured in this fashion should bear very low interest rates, since they would be issued by the ECB, and thus as safe as "money" in euros—actually safer than money, since in Europe as in the U.S., most money is a liability of commercial banks, created by the banks, while the Eurobonds would have the full backing of the ECB. The allocated funds to member nations would be distributions from a common central bank, not loans, and would not create repayment burdens for any country. These Eurobonds would be another truly pan-eurozone financial instrument, in addition to the euro itself. The bonds would not increase the money supply (M1 or M2), since investors would use money to purchase the bonds. And, in ways similar to the U.S. Treasury market, there would always be balance in the overall euro financial system, regardless of amounts of investments in individual countries.

---

[6]Alternatively, they might be perpetual bonds with no maturity but with classes of bonds with different periods for interest-rate reset: some with rates reset to the market every three months, some every year, etc. The ECB could have the option to buy bonds in the market and retire them, and holders of the bonds could have the right to put them to the ECB at a discount, in exchange for euros—although that would be a highly unlikely event. In any case, interest could be paid through further issuance of Eurobonds, or in euros, by the ECB, which would earn income from its reserves.

Although each country would still have to manage its own budget within some agreed guidelines and could issue some bonds in its own name, these Eurobonds would be available to support the eurozone during weak economic periods, and prevent recessions from becoming worse.

Summary: Myth #6, "If the U.S. does not get its fiscal deficit reduced soon, then U.S. Treasuries will face the same problems as securities issued by Greece and Ireland," is **false**; it does not reflect the nature of the U.S. financial system. Treasuries are not like "debt" in the personal sense of the word. The varying opinions about limits on ratios to GDP in the U.S. are not well founded; there is no definable limit on the amount of Treasuries in the U.S. financial system. It is important for the U.S. to promote a reasonably balanced structural budget during periods of strong economic activity over the long term, but that is a different matter: the U.S. financial system, including funds for Treasuries, is always in balance, regardless of the deficit. Investors receiving U.S. dollars for maturing Treasuries *must* put the dollars in the U.S. financial system; they could either buy new Treasuries or leave the cash in U.S. bank deposits—or buy another U.S. dollar asset, which would leave the seller of that asset with the same two alternatives. Unlike euros, which can be invested in any eurozone country, U.S. dollars are always invested in the U.S. financial system, and Treasuries are the safest of all forms of financial assets for U.S. dollars.

Chapter 7

Do American Earners Really Save So Little?

This topic is also a form of common misunderstanding: it is widely believed that Americans save very little of what they earn. But in fact, personal saving in the United States has been much more substantial than generally regarded.

In dissecting this widely stated belief, we take a different approach than was used for the Six Myths addressed in the previous chapters, which are analyzed and dispelled by following the real flow of money through the financial system. Instead, this issue requires us to look at how commonly used figures are prepared and then used in ways that may or may not be fully meaningful. This matter is included here partly because it is closely related to the Six Myths: we often hear statements to the effect of "Americans hardly save at all; they need to significantly increase saving in order to have a balanced and healthy economy." Such statements seem to influence people's thinking about spending, and lead to serious misconceptions about economic policy. This chapter explains why such statements are unfounded, overstated, or at the very least highly questionable, and not really relevant to the key economic issues affecting the United States.

Two related issues are addressed through examination of economic figures for the U.S. between 2007—just before the latest recession—and 2009, when the recession officially ended. First is how the widely quoted figures on the percentage of U.S. personal Saving would look if adjusted to reflect more normal usage of the term "saving." And second, to understand how personal Saving increased during the recession, as GDP and employment fell. That line of inquiry also leads to an increased understanding of how reductions in taxes plus increased government outlays bolstered personal Income during the recession, and prevented it from becoming more severe.

Inside "Personal Saving"

Personal Saving in the U.S., as officially reported, increased as a percentage of Disposable Personal Income during the recession of 2007-09: from 2.4 percent for 2007 to 5.1 percent for 2009. This ratio had been running at about 3 percent for several years previously; it stayed essentially stable, at 5.3 percent, in 2010. So, using these figures, many people have concluded that personal Saving by Americans, at about 2 percent to 5 percent, is too low for healthy economic development. But let's look more deeply.

As noted in Chapter 3, the basic source for most figures for Saving, Investment, and GDP in the U.S. is the National Income and Product Accounts (NIPA) published by the Bureau of Economic Analysis (BEA) of the U.S. Commerce Department. NIPA reports are quite sophisticated, useful, and well-regarded, but they approach topics in a particular way, focusing on economic value added, which is very different from the way that most people think of their monthly income or saving.[1]

A *very important* difference is that capital gains are not included in "income" in the government NIPA reports. That omission of capital gains applies whether the gains are "unrealized"—not yet sold for cash—or realized. And the amounts that people save from their capital gains are not included in personal Saving. For example: suppose that you sell some shares during the year and make a gain of $100,000. Then you decide to put $90,000

---

[1] BEA notes, in their explanatory documents, that that: "Despite its usefulness, the NIPA measure of personal saving may not be the appropriate measure for some types of analyses that focus on households and institutions. For example, analyses that examine whether households are saving enough for retirement may be better off focusing on households stocks of net wealth..."

in a savings account at the bank and spend $10,000 for a family vacation. The $100,000 is not included in personal Income, and the $90,000 is *not* included in Saving as defined in the NIPA Saving ratio. But the $10,000 of spending *does* count as Consumption, thus *negative* Saving in the NIPA figures. So, while most people would expect the Saving ratio to be increased by these activities, in fact the reported Saving percentage of Disposable Personal Income would *decline*.[2]

In addition, for reasons related to the economic basis of the tables, the taxes deducted to compute Disposable Personal Income *include* taxes on capital gains, even though the capital gains themselves are not included in income. BEA actually publishes some adjusted figures to Personal Saving rates that reflect some of the relevant adjustments, including the tax on capital gains, but those figures do not capture the headlines.

Capital gains can make a big difference. In 2007, capital gains were more than $900 billion. That factor alone would increase the Saving ratio by about 7 percentage points: a very significant difference, especially since the NIPA figure was just over 2 percent.

Also, BEA computes "imputed rent" as part of consumer spending, to reflect the economic value of housing for

---

[2]Total Income would increase if the $10,000 were spent on a vacation in the U.S., and thus provided income to other Americans. But total personal Saving could not increase as a result.

homes that are actually owned. But that is not money actually spent by people. It is an economic cost, but when real homeowners figure their monthly income and expenses they do not include "the theoretical rental value of the home we own" as part of their expenses; they do not write checks each month for theoretical amounts—they include only real, actual expenses. This is an important overlooked figure considering what a major expense housing is for most American families.

In order to get a better picture of cash outlays as typically viewed by people, we need to eliminate the imputed theoretical cost and replace it with the real monthly cash outlay of mortgage interest, along with home property taxes paid and maintenance expenses.[3] We would then see consumer outlays that are closer to the amounts that most people actually view as their real monthly expenses.

For 2007, the NIPA figures show the ratio of personal Saving to Disposable Personal Income as 2.4 percent. For 2009 it shows 5.1 percent. After making the adjustments for capital gains and imputed rent, the 2007 figure would be 13.0 percent, and the 2009 figure would be 15.5 percent. For these years, the adjusted view of people's income and saving shows *personal saving is about ten per-*

---

[3] Interest paid is included in the NIPA figures as an "outlay," rather than "expenditure," but still represents a real monthly cost to households. But NIPA includes only non-mortgage interest paid, since it has already computed imputed rent as an expense.

centage points higher than the figures usually reported. (For anyone interested in more detail, Table 2, at the end of this chapter, outlines the computations.) These are obviously big differences, and illustrate the complexity of finding simple measures for such topics. The reported figures are not wrong, they are just intended for different purposes than often used. Simply quoting the headline figures from the NIPA misses a lot of the underlying content, and can be quite misleading. Looking at the underlying data in different ways lead to the conclusion that personal saving in the United States has been much more substantial than generally regarded.

Saving and Aging

There is also an important demographic aspect to changes in Saving. As the population ages, workers in aggregate will need to directly or indirectly save gradually increasing percentages of their earnings, while a larger number of retirees are living off their savings, or "dis-saving." That is perfectly reasonable, since people save during their working years so that their savings can be used during their years of retirement; technically that is recorded as dis-saving by retired people. Whatever the retirees spend, the working population must save. Whatever the working population produces in a given year, there must be a portion of it that they themselves are not purchasing, in order for it to be available for retirees.

In 2010, approximately 13 percent of the U.S. population was age 65 and older. In addition, about 24 percent was under the age of 18. Good data about consumer outlays by age group are not readily available, but we can make some reasonable estimates to illustrate what the impact might be. If the portion of the population that is not of normal working age accounts for 15 percent to 20 percent of total consumer spending, then the adjusted personal saving ratio for working-age Americans would be computed as *more than 20 percent*—a huge difference from the generally quoted figures of 2 percent to 5 percent. Workers in America may well be saving, in total, more than 20 percent of their after-tax income. So, it is quite misleading for officials and pundits to criticize Americans for saving too little and spending too much. As explained in Chapter 3, although some families overextended with mortgages and other debt, the nation overall needs increases in spending to grow GDP and employment. And, total national Saving is really determined by the amount of business Investment in productive plant and equipment.

How Can Personal Saving Grow While Employment Drops?

Personal Saving in the U.S. *grew*, between 2007 and 2009, not only in percentage terms, but in aggregate billions of dollars. How was that possible during the crisis and big recession? Millions of people lost their jobs. Earnings were down. Did people reduce their spending so much that Saving increased even on a lower base of earnings? As we saw in Chapter 3, that is not possible. If consumer spending fell so much, wouldn't GDP have fallen even further? To help understand the key factors from 2007 to 2009, a simple summary table will be useful. Table 1 shows key changes from 2007 to 2009, adjusted for inflation, computed in terms of 2007 dollars[4]:

Table 1: Key Changes from 2007 to 2009

	2007	2009	Difference, adjusted for inflation	% change
Gross domestic product ($billions)	14,029	13,939	-508	-4%
Personal consumption expenditures	9,772	9,866	-202	-2%
Gross private domestic investment	2,295	1,547	-795	-35%
Net exports of goods and services	-713	-392	333	-47%
Government expenditures	2,674	2,918	156	6%
Note: Disposable Personal Income—NIPA	10,424	10,789	42	0%
Note: Personal Saving—NIPA figures	249	553	287	116%

Recent revisions by the Bureau of Economic Analysis show that the recession hurt even more than described in previous figures: GDP fell by 4% in real terms from

---

[4]The tables and figures used in the text have been updated to reflect NIPA revisions by the Bureau of Economic Analysis published in July, 2011.

2007 to 2009, and millions were left without jobs.[5] Personal Consumption expenditures in 2009 were $202 billion lower than in 2007, in real terms. Americans in aggregate reduced consumer spending by 2 percent. But Personal Saving, based on NIPA figures, was up by $287 billion from 2007 to 2009, in constant dollars. How was it possible for Saving to grow more than Consumption declined, while unemployment was rising?

In this situation, Personal Saving increased because Disposable Personal Income (income after tax) actually increased from 2007 to 2009, in the face of the recession. Personal Income after tax was maintained by a set of government programs: reduction in personal taxes paid, increases in transfer payments (including unemployment benefits) from government, and income from increased government spending, which in total more than offset a decline in earned income from the private sector.[6] These items together provided a significant boost for an economy that was otherwise falling rapidly.

Government Saving (the deficit) went from about negative 2 percent of GDP to about negative 9 percent, increasing by about $1 trillion. Personal Saving increased

---

[5] Spending on new homes, which declined over $200 billion, is classified as Investment and is not reflected in Personal Consumption figures.

[6] In terms of percentage of GDP: personal taxes were down by about 2.5 percent of GDP, government transfer payments increased by 2.5 percent of GDP, and government expenditures increased by about 1 percent of GDP.

as government Saving declined (i.e., as the government deficit increased). This offset between Private and government Saving is discussed more fully in Chapter 4: changes in Private Saving and government Saving, at any level of national Investment, have to be equivalent.

This background helps us understand: if the government deficit had not increased, providing additional income and lower taxes for people, it would not have been possible for total Personal Saving to increase, regardless of how much people reduced personal spending. The deficit and the increase in Treasuries issued during that time were critical to keep GDP from falling further and for enabling Personal Income after tax and Personal Saving to increase.

Total national Saving declined during this time, since Investment dropped substantially. As explained in the discussion of Myth #3, total Saving cannot increase unless the sum of Investment and Net Exports has increased. But Investment declined—about a 25 percent drop— from 16.2 percent of GDP in 2007 to 12.3 percent in 2009.[7] Net Exports improved, from negative 5.1 percent to negative 2.8 percent: NEX was less negative, meaning that a larger proportion of Americans' purchases of consumer goods and Investment goods were produced domestically, primarily as America reduced imports—main-

---

[7]This decline in Investment included residential construction as well as business Investment, but inventory adjustments are excluded.

ly petroleum products, capital goods for Investment use, and cars. But the drop in Investment was much greater than the improvement in NEX, and thus total Saving declined. There was little change in 2010: private Investment stayed about the same (except for inventory adjustments); Net Exports declined from negative 2.8 percent of GDP to negative 3.6 percent; and Personal Saving rose slightly in real terms.

Growth Requires Spending

Personal Saving in the United States has been much more substantial than generally regarded, and even while many households are still struggling with debt, progress has been made in aggregate. One measure of the overall consumer capacity in the U.S. is the household debt-service ratio of debt payments to disposable personal income, published by the Fed.[8] For the nation as a whole, that ratio reached a peak of nearly 14 percent in 2007. But by 1st quarter 2011, that ratio was down to 11.5 percent, a level not seen since 1995: that means that in total, households are now in much better shape to handle debt payments than they were in 2007. In addition, it is reported that U.S. corporations have about $2

---

[8] Federal Reserve definition: "The household debt service ratio (DSR) is an estimate of the ratio of debt payments to disposable personal income. Debt payments consist of the estimated required payments on outstanding mortgage and consumer debt."

trillion of cash on hand. So, although a number of families and companies certainly have problems, the nation as a whole seems financially quite capable of spending more on Consumption and Investment, which would increase GDP and employment; in order to have sustained growth, however, people and businesses—and governments—have to make the decision to spend.

Table 2: Personal Income & Saving: NIPA and Adjusted

	2007	2009
GDP ($billion)	14,062	13,939
salaries, income, rent, dividends & interest, pension	10,693	10,298
plus personal current transfer receipts— from government	1,719	2,138
equals personal income (per NIPA)	12,412	12,436
less personal current taxes including Social Security	1,988	1,648
equals disposable personal income (per NIPA)	10,424	10,788
less personal consumption expenditures & other outlays	10,209	10,236
equals personal saving (NIPA unadjusted figures)	249	552
NIPA Personal Saving as % of Disposable Personal Income	2.40%	5.10%
remove imputed rental of owner-occupied as an expense	1,141	1,212
replace with mortgage interest, maintenance, prop tax, etc.	834	863
A equals personal saving without treating rent as consumption—before capital gains	556	901
Personal Saving (adjusted for imputed rent) as % of Disposable Personal Income	5.30%	8.40%
B capital gains (tax on capital gain is already in the tax line)	914	914
add capital gain net income to DPI, so DPI becomes:	11,338	11,702
Personal Saving (adjusted, including capital gains): lines A+B	1,470	1,815
Personal Saving (adjusted, including capital gains) as % of Disposable Personal Income	13.00%	15.50%

Sources: BEA; 2007 capital gains from IRS, 2009 set equal to 2007. *A small further adjustment could be made for the imputed net rental income included as part of personal income, but the difference is immaterial.

Chapter 8

Economies Stuck in the Slow Lane

As we know too well, economies can become stuck in very slow modes with persistent high unemployment. The key questions are "Why?" and "What can be done to help?" In light of our previous analysis of commonly misunderstood issues, we can step back to put more perspective on the economic malaise currently weighing on America and many countries in Europe. As we saw in Chapters 3 and 7, economies can easily settle into combinations of Consumption, Investment, Government expenditures, and Net Exports that produce a GDP well below capacity, and with significant unemployment. This situation will not improve until at least one of the components increases spending on a sustained basis. This is an extremely important, but often ignored, aspect of real-world economies; this reality is particularly avoided with regard to government outlays, in light of great concern about current deficits and levels of Treasury securities outstanding (government "debt"), which are misunderstood and exaggerated, as explained in the discussions of the Six Myths. Chapter 9 presents a stark contrast with the economy of China, which continues to grow strongly, unburdened by the Six Myths.

Structural matters, such as labor flexibility and balanced regulation, have important effects over time. But even an economy with those factors in check can go through periods of strong economic activity with low unemployment, then get stuck in a prolonged period of slow growth with high unemployment, as has happened in the U.S. and parts of Europe.

When consumer spending falls, or business Investment falls, income must fall in tandem, since people are paying for fewer goods and services, and that means less income for people and companies producing the goods and services. If Investment increases, such as for purchases of machinery, that would help personal Income and cause a corresponding rise in Saving, but that happens because companies choose to invest in production, not because people are trying to spend less. Companies generally make that kind of commitment when they see or expect a rise in demand for their goods or services.

The term "stimulus" was used with some regularity during 2008 and 2009—although it is now in disfavor—to refer to government programs in three main areas:

transfer payments (notably unemployment payments), tax reduction, and spending on government projects, such as infrastructure. A key problem in perception and understanding lies in the interpretation of the term "stimulus." One implication of the word was that the government actions would not only provide temporary direct support, but would spark an ongoing flame that would grow and continue well beyond the period of the government actions. Some people expected something like lighting a piece of kindling, which would in turn ignite the larger logs in the private sector fireplace, producing a fire that would continue burning long after the kindling was gone. But the only way that can happen in an economy is if the kindling sets off a *sustained* increase in spending, in Consumption and/or Investment. Otherwise, "stabilization" is a much better term that "stimulus." Without a sustained increase in private sector inclinations to spend, government programs can still be a big help in filling in some of the decline in GDP during the slow periods. There is some automatic stabilization built into existing programs, but additional stabilizing programs are needed to fill in for declining consumer and business spending during a recession, or during slow recovery, or when an economy shows serious signs of falling towards recession.

During the recent recession, as discussed in Chapter 7, stabilizing efforts did kick in. Without the help of the

roughly $1 trillion added to Personal Income from trans-
fer payments from government, tax reductions, and increased government spending, the decline in real GDP
from 2007 could well have been more than 10 percent,
instead of 4 percent.[1] The government programs, both
those automatically engaged from existing programs and
new actions, acted as stabilizers. But as soon as some
of those programs are over the economy will fall back
again, unless spending increases on Consumption and/
or Investment, and/or increases in exports.

As explained in Chapter 5, it is critical to separate the
rationale for long-term deficit management from the current slow economic conditions. Government spending
now, and for the next year at least, is needed to reduce
unemployment, even as we plan for reductions in government outlays expected 10 or 20 years from now. And,
as discussed in Chapter 5, government spending now,
including for infrastructure, education, and defense and
health technology, is not a sign of poor fiscal management. Quite the opposite: increased spending at this time
is a highly responsible policy that will help now and
with future productivity, rather than creating big burdens
for the future.

The common focus in Washington on cumulative defi-

---

[1] A much more thorough analysis, with similar conclusions, was
published by Alan Blinder, Professor of Economics, Princeton Uni-
versity, and Mark Zandi, Chief Economist, Moody's Analytics: "How
the Great Recession Was Brought to an End", July 27, 2010.

cit reductions over 10 years misses the key underlying logic. The challenge for future budgets, as explained in Chapter 5, revolves around the deficit in a particular year, perhaps 10 or 20 years from now, when the economy might be especially robust. As explained in Chapters 5 and 6, the total amount of Treasuries outstanding is not analogous to personal debt or to the conditions in the eurozone. Regardless of what targets one prefers for percentage share of GDP for government revenues and outlays in those future strong years, the cumulative change in deficits and Treasuries between now and then is not the issue. In fact, premature reductions in the deficit during slow times can put the economy in a weaker position for the future. Over the years, there will likely be times when the economic tools provided by deficits will be quite important. To take away the ability to use deficits during weak economic times would be akin to asking a plumber to work without a wrench.

Concerns that the tax reductions and government spending during the financial crisis "did not help" are reminiscent of a person, taken ill, who needs medication over a period of time while the body regains health and strength. If the medication is prescribed for 30 days but is cut off after only one week, the person would likely not yet be healthy—but that was because the treatment was curtailed too soon, not because it could not help. This does not mean that the government has to be more intrusive or controlling in the private sector—it just means that, during slow times, government needs to put more money into the hands of the private sector on a sustained basis, by means such as tax reduction, unemployment benefits, and productive spending. This is not a belief drawn from ideology (actually, this author would like to see less intervention in the private sector by government at all levels)—it is a practical matter supported by the logical flow of money. As noted in Chapter 3, when there is little reason to expect increases in spending by consumers and businesses, or significant increases in exports, government must fill the void in order to avoid slow or negative growth and high unemployment.[2] As discussed in Chapters 5 and 6, the Treasuries issued to finance such government programs will not cause big problems in the future and will not require extra taxes to pay them down. As explained in Chapter 9, China has effectively used sustained government programs to fully

---

[2]Sometimes theories are put forward based on the hope that, once deficit reduction is announced, businesses will significantly increase productive Investment. While it is certainly possible that rationalization of regulation, and lower tax rates, might encourage some increases, it would be extraordinarily difficult for that to replace the GDP component of the current deficit level, which is estimated at more than $1.5 trillion for the upcoming fiscal year. That is more than the entire amount of business Investment of last year, so making up for that amount in GDP would require more than a doubling of commercial Investment. Even a 10 percent increase in business Investment would be good, but would mean only about 1 percent of GDP, compared to losing the deficit component of the GDP, running at about 10 percent of GDP.

avoid recession and to continue strong economic growth. China is working to build consumer spending into a larger portion of GDP; then, the government programs can be eased back. But China has not curtailed its programs prematurely, and the results have been extremely strong.

But, many might ask, doesn't the government need to balance its income and expense, just like a family? That is a form of myth bound to the Six Myths discussed: that assumption is actually a leap over logic, and needs to be challenged. There is no basis for assuming that what makes sense for a family applies to the nation as a whole—a type of fallacy of composition, as discussed in Chapter 3: often, though it may sound sensible, there is no logic in assuming that what applies to individual components also applies to the whole. That would be similar to assuming that if a single tree is limited in its growth, then the same applies to the entire forest. In fact, of course, the forest could expand continuously, even if individual trees cannot grow beyond a certain size. If challenged on the assertion that the federal government must match its revenues and outlays, people turn to Myth #1, about concern over dependence on Asian funding— which Chapter 1 shows to be false. Or they might turn to Myth #2, claiming that Treasury securities issued as part of the deficit would crowd out private financing— which Chapter 2 shows to be false. Or perhaps they'll go with Myth #3, suggesting that reduced spending by everyone, including all levels of government, would increase GDP—which Chapter 3 shows to be false. Or they might resort to Myth #4, maintaining that increased government Saving would create more national Saving and Investment—which Chapter 4 shows to be false. Or, in particular, people might try Myth #5, asserting that increases in Treasury securities issued create tax burdens for the future—which Chapter 5 shows to be false. There is no need to worry about paying off the Treasuries in the future and no need for increased taxes during slow economic periods when increased government outlays can help the economy; in fact, lower taxes would be appropriate parts of the deliberate increase in the deficit. And adherents to the belief in always trying to balance the budget might test out Myth #6, worrying that similar financing problems to those of Greece and Ireland might plague America if we do not stop issuing Treasuries—a claim that Chapter 6 demonstrates to be false.

None of the myths can logically support the assertion that the government must balance revenues and outlays at all times under all circumstances. Some people may argue for further reductions in government outlays even if taxes were lowered and even in a very bad economy. In America debates about such matters should be able to be conducted rationally, without illusions as to their economic impact. As has been demonstrated in the discussion of the Six Myths, none of the myths provide economic justification for such a position, and such insistence on attempting to have smaller deficits during slow economic times would carry an extreme risk of prolonged sluggish economic activity with high unemployment.

The Six Myths, which claim great dangers from deficits and issuance of Treasuries, are not only wrong, but they are dangerously harmful in a slow economy. In a time of recession or slow growth, government deficits, funded by Treasuries, are critically important components of protection to keep an economy from sliding more deeply.

Chapter 9

How the Economy of China Has Kept Growing, Unimpeded by the Myths

Deng Xiaoping, the father of the modern economy of China, famously stated, "It does not matter whether the cat is black or white, as long as it catches the mouse." That quote reflects a practical attitude about GDP growth that has supported China's economic development without fear of the myths addressed in this book.

GDP in China has been growing between 7 percent and 14 percent a year for the past 20 years. Even during the global financial crisis, China was one of the few major countries that had GDP growth, and one of the *very* few that had continued *strong* growth. In light of that, as other countries are trying to determine economic policies, it's certainly worth serious attention to understand how China's economy has been doing so well. This chapter will not attempt a detailed description or analysis of the economic programs of China, but will represent some of this author's interpretations from his experience leading a bank in China, with the benefit of numerous discussions with Chinese officials. The views expressed here are entirely his own; no official in those discussions ever stated the points as interpreted here and none have endorsed these views. And, of course, this author was not sitting in the room as Deng Xiaoping and other Chinese economic leaders planned their approaches. These views are intended to capture the economic and financing essence of the issues, rather than historical detail. The chapter concentrates on how China avoided the traps of the myths dispelled in this book that have hampered the U.S. and other Western economies, and explains how China drove on to extraordinary economic success.

This book by its nature focuses on government policies. It is important to keep in mind, however, that much of the economy in China, despite the strong role of government, is driven largely by the private sector. Business, even when controlled by a government entity, is conducted largely through corporations and millions of small and medium-sized private companies, which are oriented toward business success, growth, and competition in markets. Businesspeople are increasingly driven by professional performance and merit-based opportunities. Economic policies of the government are often pointed in their own ways toward promoting the success of the private sector. So despite the differences in the political systems, we can focus on elements of success in the economy of China that are especially useful as we look at the myths influencing policy in the U.S.

Very importantly, China has avoided the trap of Myth #3: economic leaders in China understand that their population tends to save a relatively large proportion of its earnings, but that would not make anything happen in the economy; in some ways it made the challenge more difficult, because as supply capacity was increased, growth in consumer demand was still slow. So the government took the initiative to encourage spending that would make GDP grow. In addition, China developed special means of financing government activities that amount in concept to the same thing as substantial deficit spending, but in ways that completely avoided the traps inherent in Myths #2, #4, and #5.

Some years ago, China developed what turned out to be a brilliant economic strategy utilizing government-controlled Investment and exports. Of course, we cannot know the extent to which the economic planners of the time utilized some of the writings of Keynes or other Western economists, but it seems that they were quite conscious of the concept that both demand and supply needed to be built. The strategy focused on two areas that offered great opportunity: Investment to build infrastructure and manufacturing capabilities, and exports. To support Investment, China fostered development of the private sector and utilized other mechanisms, including government sponsorship of large-scale industrial companies to build capacity, employing labor brought into developing urban areas from the countryside. The chain of transactions flourished, so that each block of spending by government entities led to a chain of consumer spending and Saving, as well as private sector development of businesses to provide goods and services along the chain.

Export was also approached in a very special way. Goods sold abroad were typically paid for in U.S. dollars; since the renminbi was not exchangeable, the government kept all the net dollars received, and distributed newly created renminbi to the firms in China that were producing and selling the exported goods. This practice was almost equivalent to contracting for the people employed in export companies to produce goods for the Chinese government, which the government would pay for in new renminbi. This provided a way to employ large numbers of workers, beyond that which could be supported by domestic demand. But the export strategy had some very important additional benefits. Of course the sale of the exports brought in foreign currency, but there were even more crucial advantages: the requirement that Chinese exporters compete in the international market meant that they developed a whole new set of skills—manufacturing and other business skills—and were constantly learning and improving technology that could be extremely valuable in the further development of the nation.

Since the government keeps all the foreign currency generated from net exports and gives the exporters new RMB in exchange, the money supply of China keeps growing. And, from the point of view of the exporters and their employees, they have increased income in RMB that they can spend or save.

The foreign exchange reserves of China are now far in excess of what might be needed to provide the safety to deal with potential international crises. Increases in foreign currency reserves are of no real use to the Chinese people unless they are used to purchase goods and services from other nations. At this point, increasing reserves are really more a by-product of the strategy of using exports as a means of employment and industrial development. Even though the government is trying to increase the role of Consumption in GDP, Investment, including infrastructure, continues to be a major component of GDP, and Exports continue to play a key role.

The Renminbi and the Dollar

The exchange rate of the Chinese yuan has been a

subject of great attention and great misunderstanding. China is accused of "intervening" in foreign-exchange (FX) markets, selling large amounts of yuan to "manipulate" down the relative value of the yuan. But, practically, that is not really how it works. The yuan is not freely traded in FX markets, so there is no international market in which China could literally intervene, in the sense that some other nations have done with respect to their currency trading. The only source for Chinese exporters to exchange the dollars that they receive in international trade for RMB is through China's central bank: The People's Bank of China (PBOC or PBC) and its affiliate The State Administration of Foreign Exchange (SAFE). The exporters need to exchange the dollars, because there is nothing else they can do with them; they cannot deposit them, they cannot go to an international market. The exporters just go to their banks, which then go immediately to the PBOC to turn in the dollars in exchange for RMB that they can actually use. PBOC sets the rate at which it is prepared to exchange RMB for dollars (within an extremely narrow trading band that it uses in dealing with banks in China). So, PBOC has set the rate; if anyone has dollars that they want to exchange into RMB, the rate is fixed. If anyone who qualifies wants to exchange RMB for dollars, the exchange rate is set. Either he accepts the rate set by the PBOC, or he cannot exchange. The only place to hold RMB is in a Chinese bank. PBOC then holds the dollars as assets belonging to agencies of the central government, which invest the dollars as described in Chapter 1. So, PBOC does not sell yuan into a market; however, it does create new yuan to give to the exporters in exchange for their dollars, thus increasing the money supply, as well as domestic demand—matters that the PBOC considers as parts of its overall monetary policies and practices.

When international commentators suggest letting "the market" set the RMB exchange rates, there is some understandable skepticism in China about letting such an important factor be set by international traders. This skepticism has grown since the global financial crisis revealed significant mispricing in the markets. A question in the background is essentially: "Why would a nation want to put its exchange rate in the hands of traders whose cousins were so wrong about subprime and other mortgage instruments?" And China has been concerned that a stronger yuan could move production to other developing nations, such as Vietnam, needlessly harming Chinese exporters.

(This book focuses on financial/monetary issues. There is another debate regarding policies, including about potential improvements in protection of intellectual property rights in China that might then promote imports from the U.S. and other countries. That is a different matter, for trade policy. This author and his son, Dan Newman, have published related

articles in the U.S. and China. Here are some key points: a stronger Chinese currency would be unlikely to significantly reduce U.S. imports, given the large differences in wage costs. A 20 percent decline in the dollar would not lead American manufacturers to switch purchase of parts from Asian to U.S. suppliers, if the ones from Asia cost 50 percent less today. The cost of U.S. imports, and U.S. exports using those same parts, would just rise, making the finished cost of those American products higher. For a weaker dollar to have any impact on imports, measured in U.S. dollars, the amount of imports must fall by more than the dollar falls. If the dollar declines by 20 percent relative to Asian currencies, and the number of goods imported falls by 20 percent, the sum of dollars sent abroad remains the same: Americans purchase fewer imported goods, but spend more on the ones they do buy. Not one new U.S. job is created, while prices rise for American consumers and businesses. Oddly, if demand for imports is relatively inflexible, the trade deficit actually increases with a weaker dollar; Americans just pay more for the same goods. And some imports resist the impact of new exchange rates. Oil imports, equal to about one-fifth of the U.S. trade deficit, are priced in dollars already. The best path to better balance in U.S.–China trade can lie not in trying to reduce U.S. imports from China, but in expanding U.S. exports to China.)

Government Financial Support Can Wear Many Hats

To support development efforts financially, China utilizes special forms of financing through banks, especially those owned or controlled by the central government. China has not been afraid to use government spending, in indirect as well as direct ways. A large amount of government-sponsored spending in China is done through companies and banks that the government controls, as well as special-purpose government entities for infrastructure development, so much of the spending shows up as Investment rather than government spending in official accounts, and does not show up in the national deficit. In the U.S., such expenditures are considered government spending, regardless of the long-term benefit to the productive capacity of the nation. China's figures reflect the views of the underlying nature of the projects, regardless of the means of financing. This classification makes a very big difference in the reported figures for Investment and government, and for the reported government deficit or surplus, but does not change the underlying substance. There is no one "right" way to classify such items, and it is perfectly reasonable that different nations take somewhat different approaches. But it makes comparisons, using standard figures, difficult. It also influences real decisions and economic programs.

For example, suppose that people in the U.S. conclude

that it would be very helpful for transportation, commerce, and efficiency to build a new bridge over a particular river. And China also concludes that building a new bridge over a western regional river would similarly be useful. In the U.S., such a bridge might well involve a toll system, under which the projected cash flows would cover the construction cost, interest, and maintenance of the bridge. In China, that would almost certainly be part of the plan. But, in America, there would be a problem of how to finance the bridge. The state where the river is located is already over its budget; the federal government could finance it, but that would appear as an increase in this year's deficit, and would be highly contested because of America's fears about Myths #2, #4, #5, and #6. Most likely, the bridge would never get built in the U.S. Meanwhile, in China, there is no concern about those myths. Engineers in the U.S. have estimated the cost of repairing and maintaining the nation's roads, bridges, and other infrastructure at about $2 trillion over the next five years, an amount unlikely to be secured. In China, it would be almost unimaginable that such projects would be ignored, especially in a time without full employment: Beijing would see that the needed labor was hired, workers would get jobs, and the country's infrastructure would improve, making it more competitive for the future. The government would have a special entity created to own and operate the bridge, and would arrange for one of the big banks to lend the money for construction to the bridge entity. The loan might be made by a 100 percent government-owned bank, such as China Development Bank, or by one of the major commercial banks that is majority-owned, and controlled and effectively guaranteed, by the central government. The bridge would be promptly built—and there would be no increase in the reported government deficit. The costs to build the bridge would be classified as Investment in China, not government expenditure. So China would have the improved infrastructure for its people and commerce in the future, while unfounded fears, prompted by the myths, would hold back America.

The intent of this example is not to recommend the Chinese approach for America. The key point is that thinking in China was not trapped by the myths; its economic leaders understand that growth requires spending, that spending can be directed to increase productive capacity, and that government can actively use spending to fill in gaps and promote the overall process.

Much of the financing was done through vehicles that are in some ways similar to "agencies" and state and municipal bond structures in the U.S. America does have some mechanisms by which funding is raised from the public without being included as part of the federal deficit, but on a much smaller scale; for example, Fannie Mae and Freddie Mac, until they got into big trouble, involved bonds and guarantees that were effectively supported by the U.S. government but were not included in measures of deficit financing. (Unfortunately, Fannie and Freddie far exceeded prudent bounds in size, credit risk, and complexity, and of course eventually needed direct government rescue.) In China, the funds raised by development banks, for example, are not counted as government "debt," even though the entities are, at least implicitly, guaranteed by the central government. Overall, that method has worked quite well. During an earlier part of the development process, some of the banks needed to be rescued by the government, but the total amount of funding needed was quite manageable relative to GDP, and the banking system is now quite healthy. China has a range of very powerful tools available to promote the stability of the banking system. Not only does the government control the regulations and their interpretation, but also the rules that govern both finance and industry, as well as local government activities. Such moves can go well beyond differing ways to reflect economic reality: they can make fundamental changes in the market, for the private sector, for the semi-private sector, and for government entities; and they can provide time for them to work out lasting resolutions to the underlying issues in a productive and stable environment.

There have also been special forms of securities issued to recapitalize several of the government-controlled commercial banks. The four or five largest commercial banks are largely owned by the government. They also comprise, in total, more than 60 percent of the total banking system. About ten years ago, in order to finance the cleaning of large amounts of problem loans at major state-owned banks (with no losses to depositors), the government issued special notes for new asset management companies ("AMCs") that purchased bad loans from the banks. Those notes had a stated maturity of 10 years; when they reached maturity, not surprisingly, the AMCs could not pay them off. So the government simply extended the maturity for another 10 years. Last year, when some of the major banks were raising additional equity through rights offerings, the government wanted to maintain its share of ownership. In order to raise the cash to invest in the bank equity, the government issued new bonds, which were purchased largely by the major banks. The banks paid cash to the government for the bonds, and government used that cash to invest in the banks. Such programs would likely raise lots of eyebrows in the U.S, but they worked in China. The banks are now quite well capitalized and hold substantial amounts of low risk-government bonds on their balance sheets. If, for some reason in the future, the banks were to need substantial additions to capital, this same approach could be used again.

If all the forms of securities were added up, the total

would be much larger than the standard reported figures for Chinese government securities.[1] But the key point is that it does not constrain overall economic programs in China. All these forms of securities are viewed as part of the overall Chinese monetary and financial system, and policymakers do not generally have strong concerns over Myths #2, #5, and #6. This does not mean that officials in China make public statements that minimize the myths discussed in this book. The financings are simply considered integral parts of the overall financial system, as Chapters 2, 5, and 6 explain for the U.S. financial system. In China the myths just do not hold back the financing for activities that the government believes should be done to strengthen the economy.

The relationships between government and private sector financing have other characteristics that might seem quite unusual in other countries, but work well in China. One firsthand illustration: after the devastating earthquake in Sichuan in 2008, there was a genuine outpouring of sympathy and support across the nation. Over two million homes have now been rebuilt, and many cities and towns reconstructed, utilizing government fund-

---

[1] Recently published independent studies estimate the total outstanding at 80 percent to 90 percent of GDP, compared to the frequently quoted figure of about 20 percent, and to about 65 per cent for the U.S. And the money supply (M2) is about 200 per cent of GDP, while the U.S. comparable figure is about 65 per cent.

ing. In addition, many schools in the area were badly damaged or destroyed and in need of rebuilding, and the private sector contributed actively to the program. Shenzhen Development Bank, which was led by this author at the time, along with thousands of its employees, officers, and directors, donated the funds to rebuild a primary school in a rural area outside the city of Chengdu. The construction was overseen by the local government, but the funds were all contributed by the bank and its employees. When the new school was completed, the bank organized a group of volunteers to go to the school to help the teachers and staff start up the school and its curriculum.

China Takes Its Own Approaches to Issues Faced by Many Nations

As noted earlier, all this is *not* to suggest U.S. try to replicate the financing approaches used in China. This book focuses on misunderstandings about government financing. The point is to understand how China views some of the underlying issues, and to use that understanding in asking questions about views common in the U.S. Many commentators, including international rating agencies, seem to address questions regarding government financing from the perspective of "world currency investors" who may choose to invest in country A or B or C. That could be helpful for an individual investor, but as explained in earlier chapters, a different view is required to look at the aggregate financing for a nation with its own monetary/financial system. Inside China, all renminbi must be invested in RMB assets. China does not depend on funds raised in other currencies. Similarly, as explained in Chapter 1, the U.S. does not issue securities in currencies other than the USD, and all U.S. dollars must be invested in USD assets. Even if one investor sells dollar assets, the new owner of those dollars has to invest the dollars in the U.S. financial system. In both the U.S. and China, at the end of every day the financial systems balance, including all government financings: all RMB and all dollars and all securities have a home for the night; U.S. Treasuries and Chinese government securities are the safest investments for funds in their respective currencies.

During the period of global financial problems since 2008, China has not reduced government spending nor substantially changed its taxation system or tax rates. The treasury issues bonds and the central bank issues securities as routine matters. Much of the funding for infrastructure development is provided by government-controlled banks, which also buy most of the government securities. China has also not been overly constrained about growth in the money supply, which has often run at a rate of about 15 percent to 20 percent per year. (In 2010, the money supply in the U.S., measured by M2, grew about 3 percent.) The money supply of China is now about 200 per cent of GDP, while it is about 65 per cent in the U.S.

The central bank and other government agencies have taken various steps when they considered them appropriate to help control inflation, which periodically rises for one reason or another. Sometimes inflation has increased largely from international changes in supply/demand for crops or commodities, and China has typically addressed those issues in its own specific ways. If the combination of Chinese exports and Consumption and Investment grow sufficiently so as to put pressure on capacity, the government has shown it can take various steps to slow down the infrastructure development that was planned to help a slow economy. Such government actions often include administrative limits on the growth of bank lending; in China, such limits applied to individual banks can be far more effective at slowing loan growth than conventional Western indirect approaches such as raising interest rates. Interest rates are controlled within bounds by the central bank, which works to aid the stability of the banking system.

In late 2008, when the world was facing a financial crisis, and it was not clear how much it might spread to China, the nation embarked on a *big* spending program, largely infrastructure development, amounting to about 4 trillion yuan over a two-year period: more than 13 percent of the annual run-rate of GDP. (The not-quite comparable program in the U.S. amounted to about half that size, relative to GDP, including tax reductions.) The picture seemed clear, unimpeded by fears from the myths: exports were declining; Consumption and private sector Investment were not going to make up for the shortfall in GDP, and were actually at risk themselves; government-directed spending of some sort was going to be necessary to avoid a potentially spiraling drop in GDP. China chose special focus on infrastructure development, a form of national Investment, financed in its own way, largely through state-controlled banks. China was not held back by fears about spending or deficits (explicit or implicit), nor deterred by fears of the special programs "crowding out" private sector financing.

Although the wording was chosen carefully, the essence of the message from the nation's economic leadership as the world faced financial crisis seemed clear: *Don't worry. We know that exports will decline, as the world faces real financial challenges. But the government in China will spend directly and indirectly in a big way, to avoid recession. If the amount of spending planned does not do the job sufficiently, then we will spend more—whatever it takes to keep the economy growing. So maintain your confidence; adapt as appropriate, but don't worry, don't pull back; the nation will get through this in fine shape.*

The program worked very well. Consumer and business confidence remained strong. Economic growth in China continued, despite significant declines in exports (due to the economic problems in most other countries), and GDP growth was quite strong (over 9 percent annually) in 2008, 2009, and 2010. Chinese banks did quite well during the global crisis.

The government knows that not all of the infrastructure projects will turn out to be economically advantageous, or necessarily even sound. But most of them will probably be fine. Will there be challenges along the way? Of course. But the Chinese economy has overcome challenges and the endless doubts of international skeptics for many years, managing to grow GDP more than 7 percent each year for 20 years, and managing through the global financial crisis of 2008-2009 very well. Freedom from concerns over the myths has given economic policymakers in China much more flexibility to deal with issues as they develop. In addition, there are virtually no exotic derivatives in China, and authorities did not allow subprime mortgages, or any mortgages with high loan-to-value ratios. The banks came through the global financial crisis much more smoothly than banks in many Western countries; the Chinese banking system is now generally strong and well-reserved, so despite occasional expressions of concern from the West, there is little practical risk to the system from problems that may well develop with some of the loans. And there is a general consensus that most of the programs for building new roads, power lines, bridges, subways, etc., will in fact be valuable for future productivity and economic growth of the nation.

That particular program is now coming to an end, and China is moving on to the next stage. For example, the government has announced the building, over the next five years, of 85,000 kilometers of freeway, connecting all cities over 200,000 in population, plus substantial expansion of high-speed railways, and construction of dozens of new airports.

It is well understood in China that, in the future, consumer income and spending will need to grow to be larger percentages of GDP, and that the demographics of the nation will be moving to an older population. These transitions present special and substantial challenges. China will move on to its next stages of growth and development, in its own ways—without being fettered by fears about the myths that hold back America.

Chapter 10

Summary and Key Policy Conclusions

This book began with a question from the Marx Brothers: *"Who you gonna believe, me or your own eyes?"* Now that we have seen with our own eyes the logic underlying six common economic myths, this final chapter recalls some wisdom from John Maynard Keynes:

> *"The difficulty lies, not in the new ideas, but in escaping from the old ones..."*

This book has logically analyzed six key concerns that have influenced and continue to influence American economic policy, while China has not been hampered by them. We have asked, "Why has the economy of China done so well, without these constraints?" In trying to understand that puzzle, analyzing each position carefully, we have reached conclusions that the Six Myths are really not logical, and are based on misunderstanding. Those misconceptions have led many Americans to advocate policies that are just not consistent with the underlying economic realities, and have been holding back America's economic growth.

Once we are free from bias of the myths, it is much easier to have thoughtful discussion and debate about policy alternatives. A number of conclusions have been noted in the course of the book; this chapter summarizes the myths and some fundamental policy implications that follow once the myths are dispelled. This book is not intended to be prescriptive as much as it is intended to free American thinking from needless constraints. Some of the conclusions from examination of the myths are not new, but they are developed in this book within a framework of finance and logic, including contrast with success in China. Some of the conclusions are highly contrary to established economics doctrine as well as counter to common public statements. In the summary below, those items are highlighted. Taken together, these analyses form the basis of an understanding of economies and growth that is very different from key views currently prevailing in the West.

Fifteen Key Conclusions from the Discussion of the Myths

1. "The U.S. depends on Asian countries to provide financing for America": **False.** Nations that run

a trade surplus with the U.S. are simply owners of U.S. dollars, which are always invested in the U.S. financial system. (See Chapter 1. This is a significant difference from established Western doctrine.)

2. "Money from savings of Asians has been flowing excessively to the U.S.": **False**. Although foreigners in net exporting countries are saving some of the U.S. dollars that they receive from trade, that is a minor portion of Saving in Asian nations. Domestic Saving in China, for example, cannot flow to the U.S. (See Chapter 1. This is a significant difference from established Western doctrine.)

Key policy implications of 1 and 2: Do not let U.S. foreign policy be influenced by the fact that some countries own USD assets. America, the largest economy in the world, fully finances itself in its own currency, and does not need the financial support of other nations.

3. "When the U.S. Treasury issues securities, they "crowd out" private sector financing": **False**. When Treasury issues bills and notes, it takes cash from the buyers, while writing checks in an equal amount to recipients of government payments. Cash moves from one part of the public to another, and the public ends up holding the same amount of money; there may be more Treasury notes outstanding, but the to-

tal amount of money in the system is unchanged, and there is no direct effect on real Saving or Investment. (See Chapter 2. This is a significant difference from established Western doctrine.)

4. "When investors buy Treasuries, corporate bonds, or stocks, they "use up" money that is no longer available for investment": **False**. *Money is not consumed*. For every buyer there must be a seller, and the money stays in the banking system, moving from the accounts of the buyers to those of the sellers. Investors make risk/reward decisions about proportions of differing assets in their portfolios, but the total amount of money cannot decline for the U.S. financial system as a result of investors buying existing or new securities. (See Chapter 2. This is a significant difference from established doctrine.)

5. "Personal Saving is computed from the totals of money that families save": **False**. The term "Saving" has a very special meaning in the economic tables for GDP, for a particular use in looking at economic production, very different from broad daily use of the term. "Saving" is a residual figure that equals the amount of economic spending in an economy that is not for Consumption or Government; it does not refer to the sum of amounts put in banks or funds by people saving money in the ordinary sense of the

word. Personal Saving in the U.S. has been generally regarded as quite low, but the headline figures miss important content, and can be quite misleading. Looking at the underlying data leads to the conclusion that real personal saving in the United States has been much more substantial than generally regarded. (See Chapter 7. This is a significant difference from established belief.)

6. "If everyone spends less, the nation will save more, and GDP and employment will increase": **False**. This is "The Fallacy of Thrift." The only way for GDP and employment to grow is if spending increases in the nation—spending by consumers, or by business, by government, or by buyers of American exports. No nation can save its way from a weak economy to healthy growth (See Chapter 3). China has used this understanding to underpin a program that successfully avoided any recession in the global financial crisis despite a substantial decline in Chinese exports to the West. The GDP of China grew more than 9 percent each year during a period when economies of the U.S. and most Western nations were declining.

7. "Efforts to increase Saving will produce more Investment": **False**. It is actually the other way around. The only way that national Saving can increase is if businesses decide to spend more on Investment in

buildings, equipment, and software. GDP and employment can decline as a result of artificial attempts to increase Saving by reducing spending. (See Chapter 3. This is a significant difference from established doctrine.)

8. "The U.S. needs more Saving in order to provide funding for companies that want to invest in new equipment and facilities": **False**. That is a common misunderstanding. The annual flow measures of economic Investment and Saving are very different from the stock of money available. Banks already have plenty of money to lend to businesses before new economic Saving is developed as a consequence of new business Investment. The misimpression that Saving provides the funding needed for productive Investment sometimes leads to perverse and harmful economic policies. (See Chapter 3. This is a significant difference from established Western doctrine.)

Key policy implications of 5, 6, 7, and 8: Economic policy needs to recognize that "saving" cannot be productive for the nation as a whole. It is counterproductive to discourage spending, by consumers or businesses or government, as fundamentally bad. The economy will be best off if individual consumers spend what they can properly afford: for some, more saving is wise; for those who can afford to spend, it will help the economy if they do spend more. Their increased spending will increase GDP and will not reduce national Saving. But without more spending of some sort, no economy can grow.

9. "A deficit indicates a failure of government to manage its finances": **False** during a slow economic time; it might be true only during a period of an overheated economy. A deficit can be an important element of avoiding or mitigating recession. (Chapters 3, 4, 7, and 8.) *This is not a new conclusion, although this book presents a particular logic for it. There are prominent economists who support the role of deficits during a recession or slow economy, while also supporting programs to reduce the structural deficit for strong economic times of the future. But often in Washington and other Western capitals, even when deficit spending is defended, it is almost with apology, as if any deficit is morally "bad" and damaging. That is False. Deficits do matter: in a strong economy, deficits can lead to inflation and waste of resources; in a slow economy, deficits are not only proper but essential. The key questions during slow times should be how much to increase the deficit, how to spend wisely, and how much and in what forms to reduce taxes.*

10. "America needs to address long-term government spending and transfer payments, including medical programs, in order to avoid serious deficits in the strong economies of the future, and it should

continually strive to make government more efficient and responsive": **True**, and importantly, those objectives are *not* inconsistent with deliberately and responsibly running deficits during slow economic times. Regulation can be made less burdensome, to enable more innovation and entrepreneurship, and to reduce waste; these steps should be helpful, but cannot be expected to generate sufficient new spending to revive economic growth. Such improvements are *not* inconsistent with deficits and the issuance of Treasuries during slow economic times.

11. "If the government reduces the deficit, then national Saving and Investment will increase": **False**. The notions that "government Saving" could cause business Investment, and that lower deficits and higher taxes could cause more Investment, is highly misleading, and interferes with good policy. (See Chapter 4. This is a significant difference from established doctrine.)

12. "Increases in government expenditure would reduce national Saving": **False**. "Government Saving" exchanges money between various members of the public, but does not directly affect the aggregate Saving of the nation. If government Saving increases, private Saving must be reduced in an equal, offsetting amount, thus leaving no net effect on total National

Saving. (See Chapter 4. This is a significant difference from established doctrine.)

13. "Issuing Treasuries to finance the deficit creates great burdens of debt for all our children and grandchildren": **False**. Treasuries are never repaid in aggregate; there is never a burden of repayment; there is no need nor plan to raise taxes to pay down overall Treasury securities. Treasuries issued by the U.S. government are very different in nature and implications from personal debt for an individual or family. (See Chapter 5. This is a significant difference from established Western doctrine.)

14. "Economies naturally rebound over time to levels of GDP that utilize full capacity, with full employment": **False**. We see the problem in many countries around the world. Economies can easily settle into combinations of Consumption, Investment, Government expenditures, and Net Exports that produce a GDP well below capacity, and with significant unemployment; this situation will not improve until at least one of the components increases spending sufficiently. (See Chapters 3, 7, and 8.)

15. "If the U.S. does not get its fiscal deficit reduced soon, then U.S. Treasuries will face the same problems as securities issued by a number of countries in the eurozone": **False**. That myth does not

reflect the nature of the U.S. financial system. Unlike euros, which can be invested in any eurozone country, U.S. dollars are always invested in the U.S. financial system, and U.S. Treasuries are the safest of all USD assets. China is a good example of a nation that has very successfully used varied approaches for financing public projects, and continues that public-supported financing, without the concerns of this myth. (See Chapter 6. This is a significant difference from established doctrine.)

Key policy implications of 10-15: Deficits have critical constructive roles during slow economic times, and substantial deficits in those times will not create major long-term problems. We would not insist that air-conditioning is always right and proper, even when the temperature falls to 30°F and heat is clearly needed. We turn on the heat when the temperature is cold. The government must spend when business and consumers have slowed spending. The example of China's major programs in 2008 and 2009 should be highly useful. A deficit stabilizes an economy in a recession, keeping it from becoming more severely recessionary. When the private sector eventually takes the steps going forward, with increases in business and consumer spending, then government outlays can be gradually scaled back. There is a range of views about the size and scope of government; those are important matters that deserve to be debated on their own merits—but not justified either way by reliance on myths about government financing. Wise spending by government during slow times can be done in ways that do not overly expand government intrusion in the private sector. Economists and political leaders can debate about the appropriate size and mix of increases in government spending and reduction in taxes while the economic temperature is cold (the economy is slow), but there is no need to shy away from big programs. In addition to creating much-needed jobs, the nation can seize the opportunity to make significant progress in infrastructure in particular—projects that are public by nature, and are often treated as Investment in countries such as China. Government can build modern, safe highway systems, improved education, and strong defense capability. Government can repair and modernize the roads, bridges, dams, electrical grids, airports, schools, and military equipment of America. And taxes can be reduced at the same time. In light of the persistent high unemployment at about 9 percent, programs amounting to at least a few percent of GDP each year for the next 2–3 years should be seriously considered, amounting to well over $1 trillion. After a few years, we hope, the housing situation will be largely resolved, businesses and consumers will be spending more, and legislation will be in place to reduce the long-term structural deficit projected for future years of full employment. Meanwhile, as explained in this book, there is no need to "pay for" these near-term increased deficits through reduced deficits over future years—a process that could well be counterproductive as the economy recovers. And the Treasuries issued to finance substantial employment and infrastructure programs during these slow economic times will *not* create big burdens for the future.

Some Implications in Other Parts of the World

Most of these conclusions apply to many other economies with their own financial and monetary systems, not tied to the currency of another country. This book does not analyze other national economies, but there are a few relevant observations that deserve special note:

Eurozone: The conclusions regarding U.S. Treasuries are not generally applicable to securities issued by eurozone countries, which have their own special and substantial challenges, as described in Chapter 6. The conclusions about Saving, Investment, and the need for spending should apply in any case.

U.K.: The U.K. embarked on an ambitious program of substantial reduction in government programs, attempting to improve government processes as well as the longer-run structural deficit. At the same time it is trying to reduce the current deficit, despite the slow economy and high rate of unemployment. The efforts to make government more efficient and responsive should have long-term benefits. A stated goal is to make Britain a better place to do business, which certainly sounds good, but sheer reduction in near-term spending and deficit is highly risky for the economy over this and next year. It is not clear what will drive new spending by consumers or businesses, which will be necessary to replace reduced government spending, will be required to maintain current GDP, and will be needed to fuel growth of GDP. In the meantime, near-term reduction in the budget deficit presents very serious risks for GDP and employment.

There have been some suggestions, in both the U.S. and U.K., to create some form of "infrastructure bank" to finance projects. This would utilize some aspects of the model used very successfully by China. The idea merits consideration, but would be very challenging to implement effectively in the U.S. or U.K.

Japan: Having suffered a great natural disaster, with very significant destruction, Japan is now embarking on a program of rebuilding—and it should be a major effort. If Japan shies from fully active reconstruction out of fear over some of the myths, it would add a man-made aspect to the tragedy. This is a time when the nation needs to rise above the constraints of the myths, a time when constructive spending, without fear of the myths about spending, bond financing, and deficits, is critical for national recovery.

China: This book has looked at the extraordinary growth of China's economy as a starting point to question myths. China is already largely free of almost all these myths and, though it has its own challenges, continues to grow its economy strongly. (See Chapter 9.)

What America Can Learn from the Growth of China's Economy

This book has analyzed six common myths through logic that sometimes used contrasts with China as a tool to aid in thinking through questions about economic policy in the U.S. The economy of China has developed extraordinarily well, over many years, without the constraints of the Six Myths and in the face of worries raised in the West.

There is certainly no implication that all the policies utilized in China would be appropriate in the U.S.; the question was whether analysis of some of the key differences in understanding about economies and public financing could yield useful insights. There are some aspects that stand out as particularly relevant.

The practical attitude held by Deng Xiaoping, in the face of extreme economic challenges, was critical. His famous comment about the black cat and white cat, not-ed in Chapter 9, emphasized an approach of pragmatic steps for economic growth, rather than adherence to an economic ideology. American leaders could do well to think through the valuable lessons from that experience.

In America, the Six Myths are significantly interfering with practical steps to increase GDP and employment. Sometimes, leaders who really want to help growth and jobs have been misled by the myths and widespread mis-understanding of the financial/monetary system of the U.S. In other cases, a sense of dogmatic devotion to the myths has developed, based on hopes, ideology, and ra-tionalization, and without sufficient questioning and ana-lytical thinking. In particular, concern about the federal deficit has spread to an irrational fear that stymies prog-ress. Chapter 8 explains how the fears and ideological objections cannot stand up to the logic that dispels the myths. This author would be very happy to see the pri-vate sector create the economic growth and jobs that are so badly needed now; as a practical matter, that is just a wish, and pragmatic steps by government are needed, led by understanding that overcomes fear.

The financial crisis and recession in the West were driven in part by problems of excessive and unwise *personal* debt, and debt of financial intermediaries—*not* by federal "debt," not by the issuance of Treasuries. The fears about increased "national debt" have been demonstrated, in the first six chapters of this book, to be unfounded. And the burdens of those misplaced fears fall now on all of America affected by the slow economy, especially the 14 million unemployed Americans.

Now is a time to think through how to implement an American version of the attitude that China took so successfully in 2008 and 2009. Somehow, American leaders must find ways to deliver similar messages to the people of the U.S.:

• That the U.S. government will actively build and repair infrastructure, will increase other spending wisely to create jobs, and will reduce taxes so that the private sector can spend and hire more; that if the first steps do not sufficiently reduce unemployment, then more will be done; that the programs will not be curtailed until the job is done.

• That the people and businesses of America can now start to rebuild their confidence, feeling assured that the Administration and Congress will do all that is needed to increase jobs, without fear of the near-term deficit, which will undoubtedly amount to large figures, and without fear of any of the Six Myths.

• That there will be challenging decisions, of course, about how to spend wisely and reduce taxes appropriately, but that the decisions will be made and the steps will be taken, without undue delay.

- That in the future, once the private sector has regained more strength, and only after unemployment has fallen substantially, then many of the special government programs will be gradually eased back.

- That these programs are not driven by any ideology, but are practical steps to develop growth and jobs, without fear of the myths.

The United States of America has weathered a major storm, and is now gradually moving on. But we Americans have a great opportunity to grow much more strongly, and to build a far better future. It is within our own abilities, but only when we free ourselves from the myths that have been holding us back.

About the Author

Frank Newman has had a very unusual career, including 30 years as a banking executive in both the United States and China, and as a senior official of the U.S. Treasury Department.

He recently completed five years as Chairman of the Board of Directors and CEO of Shenzhen Development Bank, China. In 2005, SDB, a national listed bank with operations in 20 major Chinese cities, was seriously troubled. After a US-based private equity firm purchased about 20 per cent of the bank's shares, Mr. Newman led a team that turned the bank around substantially, making it healthy and highly profitable—with no government funding or guarantees. After the successful sale of the major interest in the bank, he took on the role of their independent Senior Advisor.

Previously, Mr. Newman served as Chairman and CEO of Bankers Trust, a major international bank based in New York. When Mr. Newman was asked to join BT, it was unprofitable and facing substantial business, regulatory, and legal challenges. He led a program of resolution and recovery to create a broader, profitable business base, leading to the successful sale of the bank with a strong return for shareholders.

From early 1993 through late 1995, Mr. Newman served as Undersecretary, then Deputy Secretary of the United States Treasury Department. As Deputy Secretary, Mr. Newman was the number two official of the Department and represented the Treasury on a broad range of issues domestically and internationally, including economic and banking policy. He also served as Chief Operating Officer of the Department. Upon completion of his service with Treasury, he was awarded the Alexander Hamilton Award, the Department's highest honor.

Prior to his government service, Mr. Newman served as Vice Chairman of the Board and Chief Financial Officer of BankAmerica Corporation, San Francisco. Mr. Newman was a senior member of a new team in 1986 who led the then- troubled bank to substantial recovery and success—without any government funding.

Mr. Newman earlier served as Executive Vice President and CFO of Wells Fargo Bank. He also served as a director of Korea First Bank—then controlled by a US-based private equity firm—as the bank recovered from substantial problems to become healthy and profitable.

Mr. Newman has served as a director of a number of corporations and public-service organizations in the U.S. and other countries, including Dow Jones & Company. He is a member of the Board of Trustees of Carnegie Hall, and a member of its Investment Committee.